PRAISE FOR *THE MANIFESTATION WHEEL*

"Alan Seale's *The Manifestation Wheel* provides a thorough process for addressing any worthwhile project, personal or organizational. It can make the difference between commitment and compliance on a project."
> —Michael Wakefield, Senior Enterprise Associate,
> Center for Creative Leadership

"Powerful and insightful! Alan Seale combines spiritual wisdom with scientific knowledge to provide a practical 'how-to' guide on how to manifest one's higher ambitions. It is a must-read for anyone serious about making a positive contribution in the world."
> —Philip Hellmich, Co-Director of Individual Giving,
> Search for Common Ground

"Anyone who approaches *The Manifestation Wheel* with an open mind will doubtless reap great reward. The Wheel has been an invaluable tool both in my artistic endeavors and in the more business-related side of what I do. There is no question that anything is possible with this incredible new technology!"
> —Daniel Karslake, director/producer of the award-
> winning documentary *For the Bible Tells Me So*

"It's one thing to have an idea, a vision, to hold a possibility. It is quite another matter to make real in the world our ideas, visions, and the possibilities we see. Alan Seale takes us on a journey—it is a journey from emergent possibility to manifest reality. He forms a gentle and loving path for us take—a path full of wonder and free of mystery."

—Mel Toomey, Scholar in Residence, Master of Arts in Organizational Leadership, The Graduate Institute

"I want to live my life to my fullest potential, deeply connected to my soul essence. This book has been my compass in making my highest dreams come alive. Step by step, Alan is boldly showing the way to manifest my innate talents and how to create a strong and intimate relationship with myself and the world around me. It has taught me that to create from wisdom is far deeper and more powerful than anything I could imagine on my own."

—Tine Gaihede, Director, European Leadership Seminars

the
Manifestation
Wheel

the
Manifestation
Wheel

A PRACTICAL PROCESS
FOR CREATING MIRACLES

ALAN SEALE
AUTHOR OF *INTUITIVE LIVING*

WEISERBOOKS
San Francisco, CA / Newburyport, MA

First published in 2008 by
Red Wheel/Weiser, LLC
With offices at:
665 Third Street, Suite 400
San Francisco, CA 94107
www.redwheelweiser.com

ISBN: 978-1-57863-414-9
Library of Congress Cataloging-in-Publication Data available upon request

Cover and interior design by Maija Tollefson
Typeset in Goudy
Cover photograph © Don Bayley/iStockphoto.com

Printed in the United States of America

10 9 8 7 6 5 4 3 2

The paper used in this publication meets the minimum requirements of the American
National Standard for Information Sciences—Permanence of Paper for Printed Library
Materials Z39.48-1992 (R1997).

To the great teachers of our past,
the visionaries of our present,
and the leaders and wisdom keepers of our future.

CONTENTS

ACKNOWLEDGMENTS

There are many people to thank for their support while writing this book. The first thanks go to those who walked before us many generations back—our ancestors from ancient cultures who understood energy and how it works. Their wisdom and teachings have proven timeless. The more we are able to understand the depth of that wisdom and let it inform our manifestation processes, the greater chance we have for a world in which we can serve and honor one another and reach our greatest potential as a human family.

Thanks to Thom Blincoe, Able Rae, Brian Tegnander, Harbhajan Singh (Stephen Jen), David Robinson, and my father, James Seale, for reading the manuscript in its various stages and giving very helpful feedback.

Thanks to Michael Wakefield of the Center for Creative Leadership and Tine Gaihede, Director of the European Leadership Seminars, for your valuable feedback on the book from an organizational perspective.

Thanks to documentary filmmaker and good friend Daniel Karslake for being an ever-present model of these principles in action and to Murad Padamsee for stimulating conversations leading to deeper understanding of how energy works.

Thanks also to my coaching clients and all of the participants over the years in the Soul Mission*Life Vision and Manifestation workshops. Our work together helped me grow in understanding of the power and magnificence of this Wheel.

So many of you have used these concepts to manifest tremendous gifts for your communities and for the world. Thank you for all you are doing.

Many also thanks to my publisher, Jan Johnson, for your continued belief in my work, and to the entire team at Red Wheel/Weiser for all your support at every stage of the process.

To my dear friend and colleague Devin Wilson, thanks don't begin to express my gratitude for your walk with me in this continuing journey. And to my partner, Johnathon Pape, thank you for your unending support, encouragement, long hours of editing not just this, but all of my projects, and for your love. Together we have manifested a truly wonderful life.

Finally, thanks to you, my readers. Thank you for taking the time to learn about the principles of manifestation and for being willing to ask, "What wants to happen?" There is tremendous potential waiting to unfold in our world. Step by step, person by person, organization by organization, project by project, we can realize that potential and manifest a new way of living and being in the world.

INTRODUCTION

Manifestation is a word most often associated with mystical or magical events and beliefs. Its literal meaning is "to make something obvious, to show something, to bring something into form, or to prove something." In practice, to manifest something means to bring it into reality—to transform it from a thought or idea into an event, a happening, a result, or a thing.

Most people think of manifestation as a mysterious process in which things unexpectedly fall into place and somehow a result occurs without anyone knowing how it happens. The truth is, however, that manifestation is a natural, and even somewhat predictable, product of your thoughts, beliefs, decisions, and actions. The more these are in harmony and alignment with one another, the clearer the physical manifestation of them will be. The more dissonant and incongruous they are, the more confused or chaotic the resulting physical manifestation.

We are all manifesting our lives in every moment. Most of what happens to us and around us is a direct or indirect result of our thoughts, choices, and actions, and of the thoughts, choices, and actions of the people around us and of leaders in government and business. We co-create our realities, individually and collectively. Ancient wisdom traditions have taught this concept for hundreds, if not thousands, of years. Today, aspects of quantum theory and scientific research confirm these beliefs.

Recent years have brought a dynamic convergence of the fields of science and consciousness. One of the products of this convergence is an understanding of how miracles are possible, how synchronicities can be encouraged, and how we can manifest what we desire. This book offers you the Manifestation Wheel as a powerful, practical, and accessible tool that can help you turn that understanding into action.

The Manifestation Wheel calls you to a higher awareness of your own life, the lives of those around you, of your world, and of what is possible. In this book, you will learn to use this powerful tool to step beyond your personal desires and tap into the realm of "what wants to happen"—the realm of your greatest potential and the greatest potential of each moment or situation. You will learn to use your intuition to look into the future for guidance. And you will learn how to partner with energy to co-create the greatest possible outcome for your dreams, goals, and projects.

This book offers you a clear and practical method for bringing your thoughts, beliefs, and actions into harmony and aligning them with your desires. You will learn the difference between lining up "things" in an effort to make something happen, and lining up "energy" so that something *can* happen. This energetic alignment creates the optimal conditions for synchronicity to occur, synergy to develop, and momentum to build so that your desired result, or something even better, can unfold.

The first time you read this book, I suggest you read the chapters in sequence. Each chapter gives you the information and steps you need to prepare for the next part of your manifestation journey. Reading the chapters in sequence will help you learn the method of the Manifestation Wheel and master this technology of co-creation and manifestation. Once you have taken several projects around the Wheel, you will begin to internalize the manifestation process and can then focus on specific chapters that relate to specific projects.

You may also want to keep a Manifestation Journal. Writing in your journal at each step of the way can help you delve deeper into some of the questions posed, and help you reflect more fully on what is awakened in your awareness. Take time to summarize your experience in each exercise, and then in each house, before you move on to the next one. This helps you internalize the fundamental energies of each house so you learn this energy technology on deeper levels. Internalizing the concepts of the Wheel leads to manifestation mastery.

The Manifestation Wheel is a technology—a method and a tool—not an end in itself. It is a vehicle for helping you realize your dreams, manifest your visions, accomplish your goals, and create success beyond your imagination. It is a roadmap, not a destination. As you become a master of the tool, the *concept* of each house or step becomes more important than the individual exercises or questions within that house. As you learn the Wheel, you will develop a sense of each house and know its energy. You will come to know intuitively what each house asks and how it is directing you. Let your intuition and the potential of your project guide you and the Wheel will serve you well.

Take your time with this book. You may choose to read it straight through first to familiarize yourself with the Manifestation Wheel, and then return to the first house and put a project on the Wheel. Or you may choose to take each step as it comes, learning the Wheel by using it as you go. Whichever approach you choose, do it with an open mind and heart. If I ask you to do something in an exercise that you don't think you know how to do, just ask yourself: What if I did know how? Be willing to suspend your judgment and give it a try. I promise that, if you truly work the Wheel, you will manifest the greatest potential of whatever you choose.

CHAPTER 1

How Manifestation Works

If we were not making such an immense effort to separate
ourselves from life, we might actually live life day to day,
minute by minute, as a series of predictable miracles.

—Peter Senge, from his introduction to Joseph Jaworski's
Synchronicity: The Inner Path of Leadership

Manifestation is a process of transforming and aligning energy
for dynamic and sustainable results. It occurs when purpose,
potential, thought, intention, belief, and action are in perfect
alignment. This alignment engenders a process of co-creation
with the energy and potential available through the greater
Consciousness.

Consciousness is the unseen and as yet unexplained source
of all of creation. It is the creating and sustaining force of all that
is seen and unseen, known and unknown, and the web of energy
that connects it all. It is pure energy. It's the glue that holds everything in the seen and unseen worlds together. Depending on your
belief system, you may call it God, Spirit, or Great Mystery. Here, I
call it simply "Consciousness" and capitalize it to differentiate it from
an individual's or group's consciousness. For example, the mass
consciousness of the society or an individual's consciousness is

not the same as Consciousness, the creating and sustaining force of the universe.

In our culture, when you have a goal or a project in mind, the first question you ask yourself is usually: How am I going to do it? You start figuring out what you need to do, to whom you need to talk, and what you must have in order to make it happen. You start from your current situation or circumstance and use your skills, intellectual knowledge, and understanding of how life works to accomplish your goal or complete the project.

The art of manifestation, on the other hand, engages your intuitive mind, which includes your intellect and rational thought process, but extends to the unseen world of energy and potential. It transcends linear time and space, greatly expanding your awareness and opening the door to a whole new world of information. In the manifestation process, while you must take certain steps and consider certain facts to achieve your desired outcome, you draw on an intellectual and intuitive understanding of energy and potential that guides you to each subsequent step. Your actions flow from a sense of "knowing" and letting the future show you the way, rather than being locked in to an intellectual plan for getting where you want to go. The manifestation process is very organic and not always methodical. You just know intuitively what needs to happen next.

Manifestation works with energy to create form rather than trying to change one form into another. It doesn't "fix" things or solve problems. It gives birth to a whole new reality or circumstance in which the problem no longer exists or is irrelevant. It's a co-creative process of unfolding potential. The potential is what wants to happen; you partner with it by creating the optimal conditions for its unfolding.

Have you ever done all of the right things to make something happen, yet couldn't get the result you wanted? And have you also wanted something to happen and in fact it did happen without taking the steps you thought were going to be necessary?

Why did you succeed in one instance and not in the other? The answer is alignment of energy. Intentional manifestation aligns your thoughts, beliefs, emotions, decisions, and actions—all forms of energy—with what you desire or with potential wanting to unfold. This alignment sets up a vibrational frequency that attracts the circumstances and conditions for the potential to become reality. You can take all of the right steps and heed the advice of all of the right people, but if your thoughts, beliefs, emotions, decisions, and actions are not in complete alignment with one another and with what you desire, you may not get the result you want—at least not in its full potential.

Quantum Physics

Quantum physics tells us that, at its most fundamental level, everything is made up of vibrating energy. That includes objects, organizations, situations, thoughts, and people. And this energy cannot be created or destroyed. It can only be transformed. The quantum field consists of energy that is pure potential. It is a dynamic, invisible web of inseparable vibrating energy patterns that encompasses the entire universe. All of creation is born out of these energy patterns, and through this invisible web everything is connected to everything else.

At the quantum level, this energy has no set form. It exists as pure potential and has the ability to take any form. Therefore, the quantum field is an energetic field of potential and possibility. Leading-edge physicists, philosophers, and spiritual teachers now acknowledge that the quantum field may be related to Consciousness. Consciousness may, in fact, be the web that connects everything within the quantum field. Some physicists acknowledge that there appears to be an unexplainable intelligence operating within the quantum field—an intelligence that moves us forward in an evolutionary process. In a 1944 lecture, Nobel Prize-winning physicist Max Planck said:

> As a man who has devoted his whole life to the most clear headed science, to the study of matter, I can tell you as the result of my research about the atoms this much: There is no matter as such! All matter originates and exists only by virtue of a force which brings the particles of an atom to vibration and holds this most minute solar system of the atom together . . . We must assume behind this force the existence of a conscious and intelligent Mind. This Mind is the matrix of all matter.[1]

This "conscious and intelligent Mind" is what I call Consciousness. Likewise, Albert Einstein once said: "Everyone who is seriously involved in the pursuit of science becomes convinced that a spirit is manifest in the laws of the universe—a spirit vastly superior to man." This "spirit" I also call Consciousness. The relationship between Consciousness, or the "intelligent Mind," and the quantum field can help us begin to understand how some of the techniques and tools of the ancient traditions work.

The tools and techniques of the ancient traditions were, in fact, their technologies. We tend to think of technology as applied to machines and industry. But the sages of the ancient traditions were masters at using the technology of energy. Quantum theory is now showing us the science behind those ancient technologies. As we perfect our use of energy technology, we discover just how advanced the ancient cultures actually were.

---

[1] From a speech given by Max Planck in Florence, Italy, in 1944, entitled: "Das Wesen der Materie." Source: Archiv zur Geschichtge der Max-Planck-Gesellschaft, Abt. Va, Rep. 11 Planck, Nr. 1797. As quoted in Gregg Braden's book *The Divine Matrix*, (Carlsbad: Hay House, 2007) p. 216.

Let's look a little deeper at energy and how it works at the quantum level. Everything at its most fundamental level is made up of vibrating packets of energy. Sometimes those packets form objects or specific ideas (particles, in the terms of quantum physics), occupying a specific time and space. In other words, the packets of energy may become organized to form a chair or a person or a concept. The energy takes a specific form that we can grasp physically and/or intellectually. At other times, the energy packets behave like waves of energy, vibrating over a larger space and time and taking no specific form. These waves are pure potential—energy that has not yet taken on a specific shape or form, but remains capable of taking any form. What causes the energy to pass from potential into form? The answer is: Your choice.

Consider that the possibilities in life are random and limitless—pure potential—until you choose one. Your choice may be conscious or unconscious, depending on your level of self-awareness. When you have a high level of self-awareness, you give careful attention to which thoughts and beliefs you energize and which ones you don't. At a lesser level of self-awareness, thoughts take on a life of their own. Where there is little or no discipline of thought, there is little conscious control of choice. Whatever thought you focus on and give energy to becomes your choice. You may think you are choosing one thing, but, in fact, if you focus thought and energy on something else, that will end up being your choice.

When you make a choice, you energize a specific thought. That choice directs the potential to manifest into form, beginning the process of changing something from an idea to a reality. For example, let's say you are going to build a house. In the field of potential, there are an infinite number of possible designs you could choose or create for your new house. Until you make a choice, theoretically any one of the infinite number of designs is possible. However, at the moment you make a choice and start to build, the potential has begun to take form. A specific design and structure is now taking shape.

You've no doubt heard the saying: Be careful what you wish for; you just might get it. This is just another way of saying that what you think about comes about because you give energy to it. Through your focused thought, you begin to manifest a result. Athletes are great examples of how thought can manifest results. There are countless stories of athletes who visualized their perfect performance, feeling every move and sensation in their bodies, and ended up winning the gold medal. We hear again and again about athletes who overcame enormous physical challenges to make the Olympic team, or about teams that didn't appear to have a chance but, through focus, intention, and commitment, ended up winning the championship.

The more self-aware you are and the greater your intuitive awareness, the more able you are to tap into the greatest potential available within any situation or circumstance. You ask: In the best of all possible outcomes, what really wants to happen here? As you perceive that best possible outcome, you can choose to "partner" with it, helping it become reality. Potential cannot become reality unless it has a partner in the physical realm. Partnering with potential means helping it "cross the bridge" from the unseen world to the three-dimensional world. Until a person or a group chooses to partner with a potential or be its steward and facilitate its manifestation, it cannot become realized in the three-dimensional world. A potential may exist, for example, for a dynamic new business to be created or a service to be provided, but until you partner with that potential and steward it across the bridge, nothing can be created.

How do you do that? As humans, we have two fundamental aspects of our being: soul and ego. Soul is the portal through which Consciousness moves into the world. It is your essence, the core of your being—through soul you recognize your oneness with all that is. Ego is that which "thinks" and distinguishes itself from what it thinks about. It is the part of you that experiences and reacts to the outside world and to others. Ego relates to all things physical and to anything having to do with the physical world—your body, your personality, your intellect, and your skills.

Soul lives both in a physical body and in the greater Consciousness. Ego lives only in the physical, three-dimensional world. Because you are both ego and soul, you can access both the seen and unseen worlds. Therefore *you are a bridge* between Consciousness and this physical reality. Through your intuitive mind, the mind of soul, you can tap into Consciousness to discover the potential that is waiting to unfold through any particular situation or circumstance. The potential itself becomes your first partner for co-creation. As its partner in the physical dimension, you commit to being its steward and invite it to cross the bridge with you into physical reality. You then bring your thoughts, intentions, beliefs, choices, and actions into complete alignment with that potential in order to create the optimal conditions for it to manifest in form. We will use the Manifestation Wheel to facilitate this process.

Universal Laws

Why is the alignment of energy so important? We live in a holographic universe. A hologram is a pattern that is whole and complete within itself, while at the same time containing the essence of a larger pattern that is whole and complete within itself, which in turn contains the essence of a larger pattern that is whole and complete, and so on. In a hologram, every part contains the essence of the whole. The effect of a holographic universe can be understood through the simple metaphor of mirrors reflecting in each other. At some point in your life, you have probably stood in front of a three-way mirror in a clothing store or tailor's fitting room and seen how, in the mirror's reflection, the image of your body is reflected an infinite number of times. Using that memory as a context, imagine that you are completely surrounded by mirrors—six panels around you as well as a mirrored floor and ceiling. The image of your body is now reflected in every direction out to infinity. This is a very simple metaphor for a holographic universe. Whatever the essence of the center object may be, it is immediately reflected out to infinity through the endless mirrored reflections. Any change in the essence of the center object is instantaneously reflected out to infinity.

You are the center of your own holographic universe. It is your energy vibration that is actually reflected or, perhaps more clearly stated, broadcast out to the universe. Whatever you think, intend, believe, choose, and do is instantaneously broadcast as an energy vibration. If your thoughts, beliefs, choices, and actions are aligned with one another, they create a strong signal. If they are not aligned, they create a weak or conflicted signal. As the message is broadcast, it attracts thoughts, beliefs, people, circumstances, and situations of a similar energy.

What scientists now call the holographic principle was understood in the ancient Egyptian and Greek mystery schools as the Laws of Mentalism and Correspondence. The Law of Mentalism states that everything exists within the mind of God/Consciousness, and God/Consciousness exists within the mind of everything. This is simply another way of saying that the whole contains all of the parts, and the parts contain the whole. It means that every one of us exists within the greater Consciousness *and* that Consciousness exists within us. Therefore, you are born with the ability to access Consciousness and all its potential and possibility because the essence of it is within you. You just have to practice and develop that ability so that tapping into Consciousness becomes your way of life.

The Law of Correspondence states: As above, so below; as below, so above. This law is another way of saying that your thoughts and actions are mirrored in the universe and mass consciousness, and that what happens in the universe and mass consciousness is in some way mirrored in you. This means that, if something exists as potential in Consciousness, there is already a seed for it in the three-dimensional world. It cannot exist in one realm without existing in all realms. Furthermore, if it exists in your imagination, then there is a seed of that potential already planted in both the three-dimensional realm and in the realm of Consciousness. Hence, Walt Disney's famous dictum: If you can dream it, you can achieve it.

This is also evidenced in how new ideas become realities. When people have a brilliant idea and keep thinking about it, they feed a lot of energy to that idea. The more they focus on it, the more the potential starts to take form and structure in consciousness. If they don't take action, however, soon someone else will grab that same idea out of consciousness and begin to manifest it. It was just waiting for someone to become its steward and help it cross the bridge into the physical world. As above, so below; as below, so above.

There are two other laws that are important to the process of manifestation: The Law of Vibration and its subsidiary law, the Law of Attraction. The Law of Vibration tells us that energy is in constant motion and has a vibrational frequency. The Law of Attraction tells us that like attracts like—in other words, vibrational frequencies always attract similar energies. Your thoughts, intentions, beliefs, choices, and actions are all energies vibrating at particular frequencies, and they will attract similar energies.[2] This is why alignment of energy is the key to manifestation.

[2] For more on the universal laws as codified in the ancient wisdom traditions, see *The Kybalion* and my second book, *Soul Mission* Life Vision* (Boston: Red Wheel, 2003), chapter 5.

When your intention, thoughts, beliefs, decisions, and actions are in complete alignment with one another and with the potential with which you are partnering, you broadcast a very strong signal. The holographic nature of the universe broadcasts that signal and attracts the conditions and circumstances necessary for the potential to become reality. As steward for the potential, the stronger the signal you broadcast, the more you attract the conditions and circumstances necessary for the potential to become reality.

When you are a steward for something, you guard and protect its best interests at all times. You tend to it, listen to it, and pay attention to what it needs at every moment. Being a steward for potential requires intuitively listening to that potential all the time and letting it guide you. It means resisting the temptation to "figure things out" or manipulate circumstances to make something happen. It requires that you follow the energy of the potential. When you move into "figure it out" mode, it is easy to lose touch with the energetic essence of the potential. Before you know it, you can be engaged in a series of mechanical steps that do not contain the energetic essence of the potential itself. Then you are no longer working with the Law of Correspondence to achieve your goal, nor are you broadcasting the appropriate energy through the holographic universe. When you let the potential guide you, every thought, intention, belief, choice, and action contains the energetic essence of that potential.

Take a few minutes for this exercise. It can help you experience the difference between "figuring it out" and "following the energy."

Exercise 1: Figuring It Out vs. Following the Energy

Go to an open space, either a large room that you can walk across or an outdoor space. Stand at one end of the space and bring to mind something you want to manifest. Imagine that, at the other end of the space, whatever you desire has already fully manifested. Let where you are standing represent where you are now in your present circumstance; let the opposite end of the space represent where you will be once the potential is fully realized.

Take a few moments to look across to the other end of the space where what you desire is fully realized and think about how you are going to make it happen. Spend some time figuring out what steps you need to take—how you are going to find the money and the time and the resources—all of the things that you have to figure out when you are working on a project. Notice how it feels to be over here looking at what you desire in the distance and trying to figure out how to get there.

Now walk to the other end of the space, imagining that you are walking across a time warp. Stand in the place and time in which what you desire has been fully manifested. In this place, everything has been accomplished; the dream has now become reality. What you wished for is now here. Take in this feeling. Look back across to the other side of the room where it is still a dream or desire. Reflect back over the distance of space and time between your dream and your realized goal. How did you get here? What happened along the way? What steps did you take? How does it feel to consider what you desire from here? Notice that every thought you have is infused with the fact that you've already manifested your dream. Take the time to go back and forth a few times, standing in the energy of "figuring it out" and then standing in the energy of "it's already happened." Which feels more alive? Which feels like the easier place from which to work?

When you stand in the place of "it's already happened," you broadcast a strong and powerful signal. Synchronicities begin to occur. Synchronicity is the experience of things falling into place in unexplained or miraculous ways. Synchronicities happen because, through Consciousness, everything is connected to everything else. They may appear to be random, but in actuality, there is a complex set of connections being made through the web. As synchronicities occur, synergy builds, momentum is established, and, in time, what you desire becomes reality in the three-dimensional world.

This is the technology of manifestation.

CHAPTER 2

An Overview of the Manifestation Wheel

Whatever you can do or dream you can, begin
it. Boldness has genius, power, and magic in it.

—attributed to Johann Wolfgang von Goethe by William H.
Murray, *The Scottish Himalayan Expedition* (1951)

Many years ago, one of my teachers, Rick Jarow, introduced me
to the Lakota Medicine Wheel, an ancient tool for manifestation.
Over the years, as I used the Medicine Wheel for projects, I
discovered its many parallels to other ancient wisdom traditions and to quantum theory. I recognized this Wheel as a
powerful technology—one that could be updated to the 21st
century and used as a tool for shifting consciousness and facili-
tating transformation. So in 2001, I began asking the Medicine
Wheel to show me intuitively how to bring it into the mainstream 21st–century world.

The result was the Manifestation Wheel, a dynamic tool
for alignment, action, accomplishment, creation, and success
rooted in the ancient wisdom traditions and the basic laws of
quantum physics. It is a powerful technique that can be used by
individuals or organizations for turning ideas into results, dreams

into reality. In your personal life, it is a powerful tool for manifesting dreams, identifying and reaching potential, making decisions, and solving problems. In your professional life, or for organizations and businesses, it is a highly effective tool for strategic planning, project development and management, and team building. It provides a practical, step-by-step model for shifting global consciousness one person and one organization at a time.

The Manifestation Wheel is a technology for aligning thoughts, intentions, beliefs, choices, and actions with the energetic essence and potential of a project or vision, as well as the positive evolution of consciousness. It can be used for any project, large or small. On a personal level, it can help you discover the greatest potential waiting to unfold, resolve conflicts and personal resistance related to a project or vision, mastermind possibilities, and find needed resources.[3] As you work your way around the Wheel, you learn to access the greater Consciousness, develop personal leadership skills, identify practical action steps and create a workable action plan, and learn new methods of co-creating with potential as well as with colleagues and collaborators.

For organizational or group projects, the Manifestation Wheel provides a practical and powerful system for turning ideas into results, project development and implementation, strategic planning, personnel management, and new business initiatives. You can use it to discover the greatest potential waiting to unfold within your organization and your project, or resolve conflicts and resistance to the project or vision within the

[3] Masterminding takes the creative process of brainstorming a step further. In masterminding, you intentionally expand your mind into the intuitive realm and let things come to you. You may get intuitive "hits" in brainstorming, but you often don't know how they happened. With masterminding, you intentionally open to another way of being, thinking, and exploring. You invite the greater consciousness and the energetic potential of your vision or project to participate in the conversation. See chapter 3 for more.

organization and/or team. Your group can learn to mastermind possibilities together and find needed resources by accessing the greater Consciousness. Each member of your group can further develop their personal and group leadership skills. The team can learn how to let potential guide them in creating and implementing a realistic action plan, all within a framework of co-creating with potential. Through the process of the Wheel, your group or organization can discover the bigger picture of their identity in the world and their role in contributing to future generations and the mass consciousness.

On a personal level, the Manifestation Wheel can be used for making a career change, starting or restructuring a business, finding a partner, or losing twenty pounds. On an organizational level, it can be used for projects ranging from a major marketing campaign, to a complete restructuring of your organization, to planning a company holiday party. Once you are facile in using it, some projects will go around the Wheel in an hour or less; others may take a year. It all depends on the scope and magnitude of the project.

The Manifestation Wheel is a model and guide for the inner journey of self-awareness and transformation necessary for the outer manifestation of a vision. The experiential nature of the Wheel helps individuals and/or organizations with practical planning and strategy. It also addresses internal beliefs and perspectives that can get in the way of success. The Wheel not only calls forth the greatest potential for your vision or project, it also ensures that every step of the process is informed by the greater potential. Through the holographic principle, the Wheel ensures that every planning and action step you take is infused with the energy of the accomplished manifestation.

Although the Manifestation Wheel is equally effective for individuals, organizations, businesses, or governments, I will focus here on its personal application. All the concepts, exercises, and processes I present, however, can easily be adapted to organizational or group applications, sometimes by simply changing "I" to "we," or "me" to "our organization." When you adapt the exercises and processes of the Wheel to your organization or business, it can be an invaluable planning tool. Chapter 12 offers a summary of the concepts, considerations, and processes of each house of the Wheel for organizational applications.

The Journey Around the Wheel

The Manifestation Wheel is made up of eight steps or "houses," as they were called in the Lakota Wheel. Each house addresses a different aspect of the alignment necessary for manifestation to occur. By the time you have made your way around the Wheel and invested time and energy in the questions and concepts of each house, you have done both the inner and outer alignment work necessary to bring your vision to reality.

The four directions honored in the Native American traditions—east, south, west, and north—provide a context for the houses (see figure 1). Native Americans enter their ceremonial circles from the east. And so we enter the Manifestation Wheel from the east where the Sun rises, representing birth, new possibilities, and new beginnings. The houses found in the east are Intention and Peace. The south represents passion, heat, growth, and development. Here we find the third and fourth houses—Energy and Guidance. The west, where the Sun sets, represents intuition and wisdom. Here we find the fifth and sixth houses—Empowerment and Action. Finally, in the north, which represents accomplishment, introspection, reflection, and rest, we find the seventh and eighth houses—Surrender and Legacy.

A second context for the journey around the Manifestation Wheel can be framed by five basic questions that must be answered

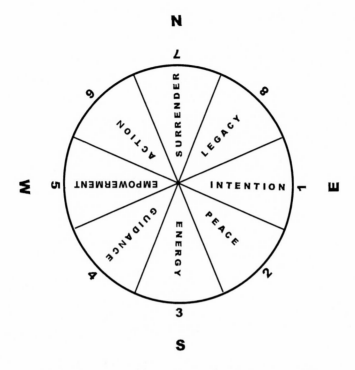

Figure 1. The eight houses of the Manifestation Wheel.

to accomplish any goal, achieve the greatest potential of a project, or to manifest a dream (see figure 2 on page 18):

- Who am I in this project and why am I here?
- Where am I going and what am I doing?
- Why?
- How?
- Is it sustainable?

The journey around the Wheel takes you deep inside these questions to bring focus, clarity, and alignment. Through the

Wheel, you clarify your position and role in the project and your reasons for being involved. You clarify the project itself and the direction it wants to take. Motivations become clear and aligned. You co-create an action plan with the potential itself and "consciously" implement the plan. And you ensure the sustainability of the project and confirm that the project can sustain those involved throughout the process. Through the Manifestation Wheel, you maximize skills, talents, and purpose, and tap into Consciousness to call forth the greatest possible outcome of your manifestation project.

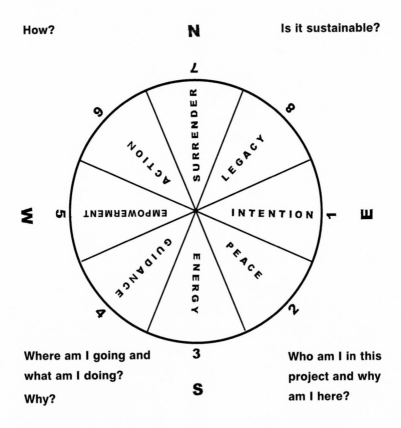

Figure 2. The five questions of the Manifestation Wheel.

Let's take a quick tour around the Wheel within the context of these five questions to give you a sense of the journey.

East: Who am I in this project and why am I here?

In the first house, Intention, you clearly name what you are putting on the Wheel. What do you intend to manifest? This may be a goal or project, a decision, the solution to a problem, a new fundraising or product launch, a new marketing initiative, or a restructuring of some aspect of your life or work. This house calls you to be absolutely clear about what your intention is and where you are as you begin. Here you clarify your role in this project or dream and how it relates to who you are in the world. It asks for your total commitment to the manifestation process, and to the personal stretching, learning, and growth that may be required along the way.

In the second house, Peace, you uncover and identify any conflicts around or related to your vision. Is there any part of you that is not in alignment with this vision? Is the vision in alignment with your soul and your values? If there is conflict with the vision or project on any level—either in how it is being accomplished or in the outcome you seek—that conflict drains away energy. These conflicts must be resolved before you proceed with the project. If every part of you is not completely on board, it will be difficult to sustain the necessary energy to pull off the project or accomplish the goal.

South: Where am I going and what am I doing? Why?

The third house, Energy, invites you into a big strategic masterminding session. Here you consider possible directions, goals, objectives, and scenarios for the project. You build enthusiasm and energy, find your true motivation, and mobilize the necessary forces and energy. You identify resources and tools that will be required for the project to manifest. You consider who else you must motivate and excite. While the temptation may be strong to create a full-blown action plan at this point, that would be premature. In this house, you create an energy focus and a sense of momentum for the project. That energy and momentum will continue to build in the next two houses, resulting in a much stronger foundation and clearer vision by the time you create and implement your action plan in the sixth house.

When you begin a manifestation project with clear purpose and intention, add thoughts and beliefs that are in alignment with that purpose, and then add energy and vitality, the result is a solid foundation for incredible success. This is what you accomplish in these first three houses.

The fourth house, Guidance, invites you into a visioning process. Here you tap into the future to learn more about the greatest potential available through your project. This house is not about forecasting the future. It is about asking the future to show you what the full manifestation may look like in its greatest potential. The purpose of this house is to awaken intuition and learn how it and intellect can work in tandem to guide a strategic manifestation process. Very often in this fourth house, you begin to formulate an even bigger picture of your vision or project.

West: How?

The fifth house is Empowerment. Here you consider how this project or vision calls upon everyone involved to be their best and shows how the project will serve them. You consider the leadership skills that are needed and develop or call forth those skills from all of the players involved. You look at who you and everyone involved in the project are becoming through its manifestation and evaluate how that feels. You consider how the project can feed the lives of everyone it touches.

At last, the sixth house brings us to Action. In this house, you clearly identify your strategies and directions, your goals and objectives. You create an action plan and put it into motion. What makes this action plan different from a conventional plan? Your continued awareness of who you are as you execute the plan and your acknowledgment of what is driving the action. Are you and everyone involved continuing to step into your greatest personal potential through this action plan? Is the plan being driven by personal desires or by potential? What wants to happen in the greater scheme of things? In this house, you seek the help and counsel of others who can guide or assist you in powerful ways, and you estimate time frames for accomplishing the vision.

North: Is it sustainable?

The Manifestation Wheel teaches you about the process of co-creation with others, as well as with potential and the greater Consciousness. The seventh house, Surrender, takes the co-creation energy even higher. You have done your work; you have put your action plan into motion. At a certain point, you must release your project to the greater Consciousness and trust that synergy will unfold and synchronicities will occur. The project now has a life of its own. Things happen that you can't control and possibly had never imagined. Your role in this stage of the co-creative process is to respond to what happens as the project takes on its own life. You must continue to be a steward for it, follow its energy, and play within the synergistic processes. You must surrender to the unseen forces and learn to step beyond the bounds of rational thought. In so doing, you enter into a more dynamic, intuitive, co-creative partnership.

The last house of the Manifestation Wheel is Legacy. Here you consider the sustainability of your vision and its impact on generations to come. You consider not only whether this manifestation project will benefit you and your family or organization and community, but also whether it will benefit the greater human family. How are you contributing to the future? What are you creating for your grandchildren's grandchildren? Is the process and outcome of your project in harmony with the positive evolution of humanity? The ultimate question is: In what ways are you leaving the world a better place through this manifestation project?

The Manifestation Wheel expands your awareness of your ongoing contribution to your global community, now and in the future. It helps you understand its vibrational legacy—the legacy you create through your thoughts and feelings as well as your actions. When you bake bread or brew a fresh pot of coffee, the aroma permeates the entire house. In the same way, the energy patterns of your creations, thoughts, and actions permeate the universe and mass consciousness. Regardless of whether your project is large or small, it is still an energy system that reaches out into the mass consciousness and spreads its vibration. Therefore, it is important that your intention and completed project be in harmony or alignment with what you want your legacy to be.

A Circular Process

The Manifestation Wheel is a circular process. The final step in each house is to return to the previous houses to make sure that everything remains in harmony and alignment. You may find, for example, that as you work in the second house, you simply cannot come to peace with a particular aspect of your project or intention. Therefore, you must return to the first house and make whatever revisions are necessary in your intention so you can be at peace with all of it. Or you may find that, as you look at empowerment in the fifth house, some of the goals you set in the third house diminish the empowerment of certain individuals or groups. In this case, you must return to the third house and revisit those goals.

Harmony and alignment are essential in the manifestation process. Where there is discord, synergy and synchronicity are blocked. Synergy and synchronicity are the vehicles through which manifestation occurs. Again, manifestation is not about making something happen. It is about setting up the conditions of alignment and harmony that will attract a particular outcome. Your project, your personal integrity, your soul, and the potential that wants to unfold must all be in alignment in order to manifest the greatest outcome. So before leaving each house, you must check in with all the previous houses to see if your work has further illuminated the project or intention and resolve any conflicts that may have arisen.

As you complete your trip around the Wheel and return to the first house, you will find that you are now in a very different place with your project or vision than you were when you began. Perhaps your project is complete and you are moving on to the next goal. Or perhaps your project is continuing in another phase. In either case, when you reenter the first house, you set new intentions and make new commitments for the next part of your journey.

Whatever you choose to put on the Manifestation Wheel, the process will take it to its grandest scale. You will also find that the process of the Wheel has many layers. As you create your action plan, you may realize that some of its components or steps would benefit from having their own Wheel. Or you may realize that another project must be completed before you can continue your current one. Put that project on its own Wheel and work your way around. When it is complete, return to your initial project and continue with it. All of this is to say that you may end up having several Wheels going at once for the same project—a master Wheel and its sub-Wheels.

Much of the process of the Wheel relies on you allowing the work of each house to be present in your thoughts throughout the day. You will find yourself coming to new revelations as you ponder each house. Take time to meditate or reflect each day on your project and the house where you are currently working and you will be amazed at what can happen.

When you take a project around the Wheel, you go through both the inner and outer processes of manifestation. Your internal processes create the energetic field in which the outer manifestation occurs. Just because you have gone through all eight houses, however, does not mean that your project is complete. It means that everything is now in place for the project or vision to manifest. It may take some time for all of the pieces to fall into place. Your responsibility is to maintain harmony and alignment of energy so the potential can unfold in its own time.

Another universal law, the Law of Gestation, tells us that all things come in their own time. It takes nine months for a baby to develop to the point where it can live outside the mother's womb. A cake will not be done any sooner than the time it takes for the necessary chemical reactions to occur in the oven. So it is with your manifestation projects. It can take time for things to fall into place. The more complex a project, the more people and "puzzle pieces" involved, the longer the gestation time is likely to be. Therefore, you must always be patient in the manifestation process. Your time and its time may not be the same.

Does taking a project, goal, or dream around the Wheel guarantee that it will manifest? We all know that there are no guarantees in life. Remember that manifestation is not about making something happen; it is about setting up the optimal conditions that will allow it to happen. There are many factors that contribute to any outcome, as well as many "votes" on what that outcome should be. There is, of course, your vote—what you want to happen. There is also Consciousness, that intelligence that is the creating and sustaining force of all, which works from the "big picture" view of what wants to happen for all, not just for you. And there is the energetic focus, alignment, and desires of others who may be involved in your situation or project. Manifestation involves the alignment of all three and depends on finding the energetic flow in which all three are "voting" for the same thing.

The Manifestation Wheel supports learning, growth, and development, as well as alignment of energy on every level. That is its gift. If you commit to the manifestation process, follow it step-by-step, and let go of your attachment to a specific outcome, the greatest potential for your vision or project will indeed unfold. In the end, it is the journey of discovery and growth rather than the destination that is important. If you consider all of the questions the Wheel poses honestly and fully, do the deep inner work that is required, develop your intuitive mind, and take the actions that are called for, your journey around the Wheel will help you refine your vision or project so that, in the end, you receive a result you desire.

A few suggestions as you step into the Manifestation Wheel for the first time. I recommend that, for your first journey around the Wheel, you choose a relatively small and simple project or goal—something that you are fairly confident you can accomplish, yet something that will still be a stretch for you. Depending on the complexity of your project, you may need several days, or even a week or more, to take your project around the Wheel. You will move through some houses quickly; others will take longer, sometimes when you least expect it. That is one of the gifts of the Wheel. It assures that there are no stones left unturned, no places where the energy is not in complete alignment. Therefore, give yourself as much time as you need in each house. If you choose to spend several days or more in a particular house, read through that chapter each day and keep the exercises and concepts of that house fresh in your mind. Each time you read through the chapter and reflect on the considerations for that house, you will find new layers of awareness, discovery, and understanding.

And so we step into the first house—the House of Intention.

CHAPTER 3

House #1: Intention

Identify and name your intention.
Identify the greatest potential for your project or vision.
Commit to change and growth.
Commit to the journey of the Wheel.

As you enter the Manifestation Wheel and step into the first house, you begin the journey of bringing your vision or project to reality. Here you set your intention for what you will manifest, as well as for who you will be within the manifestation process.

In the first house, there are five fundamental things you must accomplish to set your intention and pave the way for your manifestation journey:

1. Clearly state the project or vision you intend to manifest.

2. Discover and embrace the greatest potential available for your project or vision and commit to its manifestation.

3. Discipline your thoughts and commit to bringing them into complete alignment with the potential you want to manifest.

4. Commit to the learning, transformation, and growth required to manifest your vision.

5. Commit to listening intuitively to the potential of your vision and your own inner guidance at each step of the way, and to respond to that guidance with appropriate action.

All of these things involve commitment—your commitment to your vision or project, to your personal and/or organizational responsibility in the manifestation process, and to the process itself. Your commitment is what initially gets the ball rolling. The stronger your commitment, the stronger signal you broadcast to the universe from the start. It's also a clear indication of how important this project or vision is to you. If it is not terribly important, you are not likely to do your own personal work along the way—to discipline your thoughts and actions, to work through doubts and resistance when they arise, or to learn the new skills that may be required.

Becoming a master at manifestation requires self-mastery. It requires a high level of commitment to living up to your greatest potential within any situation or circumstance. Therefore, from the very beginning, the Manifestation Wheel asks you to commit to learning, to facing challenges, to growth and transformation, and to claiming breakthroughs when the opportunity for them arises. When you start out on the manifestation path, there will be times when you can't see clearly what is ahead. There will be things you must discover as you go along. At the beginning, you may not have all the skills and resources necessary for the manifestation of your vision, or even know what they are. That's okay. The journey around the Wheel offers you the opportunity to develop these skills and find these resources. Learning and manifesting go hand in hand. This requires a willingness to change, grow, and accept that there are things that you don't know or understand. It requires that you stretch beyond your comfort zone, face fears and resistance, reevaluate beliefs and behaviors when your default settings no longer serve you, and let go of assumptions about how you think things will or should be. The potential waiting within your vision or project may have another idea, and it usually has the "bigger picture" view.

Trusting your intuitive understanding and working with energy may itself be a stretch for you. Our mainstream culture does not yet support the idea of life being guided by intuition, although that is changing. The December 2004 issue of *Fast Company*, a leading-edge American business magazine, predicted that acting on intuition would be the number one trend that could change the way we live and work in the future. When well-respected business magazines are calling intuition the number one trend, it's time for the technology of manifestation to go mainstream.

Intuitive development is greatly accelerated and enhanced by a regular reflective or meditative practice. When I am asked what form of meditation I recommend, my response is always: Whatever works! The form of your reflective practice does not matter as much as the fact that you have one that works and is comfortable for you. You know that it is working when you can do the practice daily without a great deal of resistance or procrastination. The right daily practice for you may be a form of Eastern meditation, or a walk in a serene and peaceful setting, or a jog. Whatever the practice, it should be time spent in silence—no music or conversation, just you and the silence. Regardless of your chosen practice, use it to drop down underneath your current thoughts and feelings, your perceptions and opinions, to discover who you are at your core—at the level of your soul. It is at this level that you tap into the greater Consciousness and discover potential.

If you don't already have such a practice, just close your eyes for a few minutes several times a day and focus your attention on your breath. Here is a simple tool to help you.

Exercise 2: Breathing into the Silence

Close your eyes and focus all your attention on your breath passing in and out through your nostrils. As you focus on your breath, your inner rhythm will slow down and become steady and peaceful. Within a few moments, that calmer inner rhythm will begin to affect your outer rhythm. This may take a little time if you are very tense or stressed, but be patient. Just breathe. Smile as you breathe, and your whole body will relax. That's all there is to the exercise—just close your eyes, breathe, and focus all your attention on your breath. Your body and mind will respond automatically.

Throughout your day, take a few moments to do this exercise. Your breath can be your best friend for helping you enter the silence and find your quiet center. It can help you remain calm and focused all day long. You can do this anywhere—on the job, between appointments, while working out, or while dropping off to sleep. Let your breath show you the way to your stillness and quiet.

Having a regular reflective practice will help you approach your work with the Wheel from your true, centered self, rather than from the fast pace or occupations of your day. In fact, every significant decision of your life will come more easily and clearly when you have a regular reflective practice. Here is another tool that can help you as you develop a daily reflective practice.

Exercise 3: Finding Your Point of Stillness

Sit quietly with your eyes closed and back straight. Put your feet flat on the floor or fold your legs under you. Rest your hands comfortably in your lap. Take a few deep breaths, allow your body to relax, then let your breath find its own natural, relaxed, easy rhythm. Begin paying attention to your breath as it passes through your nostrils. Bring all of your attention to that point of focus—your breath passing through your nostrils. There is nothing else in your conscious awareness except your breath.

You may notice a great deal of "chatter" going on in your mind as you attempt to focus solely on your breath. It's okay. Just notice it. Then step by step, layer by layer, drop beneath the chatter. As you inhale, imagine the floor of your current layer of awareness opening. As you exhale, let yourself float gently down to the next deeper, quieter layer. As you inhale again, imagine the floor opening; as you exhale, float gently down to the next layer. Continue this process until you come to a place of absolute quiet and stillness. You may have to pass through many layers of mental chatter and distractions before you finally reach this place. It's all right. Don't worry about how long it takes. Just keep breathing and floating down to deeper and quieter layers.

As you float deeper, notice that you begin to feel calmer, more centered, and more grounded. Feel your heart open. You are simply opening to you—your essence, your soul. You become cognizant of several layers of awareness and consciousness at once. You begin to understand on a whole new level the meaning of "still waters run deep"—that, although on the surface there is lots of chatter, the deeper you go, the quieter it gets. Take your time to float for a while. When you feel as if the exercise is complete, open your eyes.

Notice how different you feel after this short exercise. Perhaps you feel more relaxed, centered, or peaceful. Or perhaps this was hard for you because you had so much mental distraction. If that is the case, be gentle with yourself and start out by doing the first exercise several times a day for a few days. Then come back to the Point of Stillness exercise.

Practicing these simple processes daily can greatly enhance your journey around the Wheel and enrich your daily life.[4] Grounding yourself in a daily reflective practice and trusting your intuition are essential to identifying the potential within a vision, project, or situation.

Potential, Possibility, and Outcome

Before we go further, let's make clear the distinction between potential, possibility, and outcome. Potential is often thought to be a specific thing or result that could happen in the future. In truth, however, potential is pure energy that has not yet organized itself into a specific form. Potential is the driving force behind the highest levels of creativity and manifestation. It exists in the unseen realm of Consciousness where past, present, and future co-exist. There is no sense of linear space and time as we know it in the realm of Consciousness. Therefore, potential is an energetic essence that is present right now in your project and wanting to emerge. It has movement and action. Potential is what is waiting and wanting to happen. Possibility is a specific way that a potential may manifest into form—what could happen. Outcome represents the end result— what did happen.

[4] There are many books and audio programs that can help you create a regular reflective practice and develop your intuitive skills, including my first two books, *Intuitive Living: A Sacred Path* (Boston: Red Wheel, 2001) and *Soul Mission* Life Vision* (Boston: Red Wheel, 2003).

Potential: An energetic essence; energy unformed or waiting to take form; what wants to happen

Possibility: A form that potential may take in the physical realm; energy taking a specific form; what could happen

Outcome: A form that has taken shape and become "real" in the physical realm; what did happen

For example, let's say you want to manifest a new house. You begin by asking: What is the greatest *potential* waiting to emerge? The response is mostly things you expect: an open and spacious feeling, a space that nurtures your creativity. And then you are shown a potential you hadn't expected: close to walking trails in the woods. Along with the potential comes the intuitive message that you need to spend much more time in nature to balance your stressful work life and enhance your creativity.

So you partner with that potential and become its steward. You call a realtor and give her the usual list of things you are looking for in a house: style, size, characteristics, price range, easy commute to work. Meanwhile, you continue to focus on the potential of open and spacious feeling and nurture, *and* close to walking trails. The realtor shows you several houses— all *possibilities* that do, in fact, offer the realization of the full potential. You then choose the *outcome* from among the possibilities—the house that you will buy. Had you only focused on a new house of a certain style, size, and price range with an easy commute to work, you might not have received the important intuitive guidance about your need for time in nature. You might have missed the opportunity to manifest a house that was close to walking trails.

Let's look at a professional or business example—perhaps a project to launch a specific new product or service. You ask:

What is the greatest potential wanting to happen here? You discover, however, that instead of just launching the service, the greatest *potential* is actually to open the market to a new way of thinking about this entire genre of services. The *possibilities* of how you do that may include promotional campaigns, new designs for the service, public education programs, creating alliances with key opinion leaders, and perhaps the repositioning of your professional brand. The *outcome*, then, is that the new product initiative has sparked an entirely different line of services and a whole new "look and feel" for your business. When you started, it was not clear what the outcome would be, except that, at a minimum, you would get the new service launched. By focusing on the potential instead of the outcome, so much more happened.

Suppose your intention is to manifest a new job. You ask: What is the greatest potential waiting for me in a new job? The answer may be to travel to exciting places, experience great autonomy within a progressive organizational structure, and gain personal reward and fulfillment through service to others. When you focus on the potential, the energy is free to manifest the greatest possible position. If, on the other hand, you focus on manifesting a very specific position in a particular company at a specific salary with a certain job description, you greatly limit the manifestation possibilities, and the greatest potential that was waiting for you may never be realized. Furthermore, you limit the field to such a specific possibility that the odds of it becoming available are substantially reduced.

Potential, possibility, and outcome are all parts of the manifestation equation. Regardless of what you want to create, you are conditioned to start with a specific outcome in mind. This can trap you in a fixed form with fixed conditions. It can also put you in problem-solving mode or "making-something-happen" mode, giving more energy to your current circumstance or a specific outcome than to what the true potential may be.

The Potential of Pure Energy

We have said that manifestation is about alignment of energy, and that energy is the fundamental essence of everything. When energy is in its pure state, it has the potential to become anything. When it has already taken a particular form, however, it has become organized into a fixed structure. Attempting to change one form into another is like problem solving. An object, situation, or circumstance exists in one particular formation of energy and you want to transform it into another. For example, if you design a new chair and then discover that the design is flawed—the chair collapses when someone sits on it—you may try many approaches to make it better or to fix the problem. But if the fundamental design is flawed, no amount of attention to it is going to make that chair support the weight of a person. Instead of focusing on the flawed design, ask intuitively: What wants to happen here? What successful design is waiting to be created? Then let the potential show you the new design.

Perhaps you are caught in a conflict with a colleague or your boss. If you keep focusing on resolving the conflict, you are trying to change one energy structure to another. Instead, ask intuitively: What wants to happen here? You may be shown an entirely different working arrangement that would better serve everyone involved. Then focus on creating the new working arrangement, and the conflict energy is transformed into a new level of cooperation and partnership.

Manifestation starts with a vision or an idea. The vision or idea is pure energy that has not yet taken form in the physical realm. Manifestation therefore works with energy and the potential that lies within the vision. It is a process of transforming energy into form. In this first house, we therefore start with energy as pure potential, partner with it, and begin stewarding it into reality. The greatest possible form or outcome will emerge as you work your way around the Wheel.

Energy is constantly shifting and changing. How fast or slowly or obviously that change occurs is relative to the density and mass of the form, structure, or situation. The denser the form, the slower the vibrational frequency. The larger the form or the more complex the structure or situation, the longer it can take for change to permeate it. In other words, you can make a change in your own life faster than your whole family can implement that same change. Likewise, an organization with only ten members can usually implement a procedural change faster than a global organization with thousands of members.

How quickly or efficiently you are able to implement change or manifest something new depends on whether you are working with it in form—trying to change a situation or circumstance—or in potential—asking what wants to happen and then manifesting a new circumstance or situation. When you work in form, change is a slow process. Form is heavier and less pliable than the pure energy of potential. However, the pure energy of potential is very flexible and easy to shape. Therefore, when you partner with energetic potential, change and manifestation can happen much more rapidly. Just as you need potential as a source of inspiration, creativity, and innovation, potential needs a steward, a partner, a grounding force to help it manifest in the three-dimensional realm of form. As a steward for potential, you become an active participant in the co-creation of your present and your future.

This involves creating an energetic space or field of energy around your project that holds its energy and provides a safe space for you to tune into intuition, the potential, and Consciousness so you can be creative and innovative. If you are working alone, it is up to you to create and hold that energetic space. If you are working on a group project, you can assign someone on the team to be the chief steward for the potential.

It is his or her job to hold the space, to bring the group back to it when they stray, and to guard and protect the energy.

It is important to create a safe space for manifestation conversations to occur. If you are truly following the potential, those conversations may not be your typical business-team conversations or your typical chat with your next-door neighbor. They may be highly intuitive conversations in which everyone needs to feel safe to say anything that comes to mind, trusting that they will not be judged or criticized. Intuitive conversations with Consciousness and potential must transcend "in-the-box" thinking and previous contexts of what things mean and how things have been done. As stewards for potential, you are partnering with an unseen force. That's already "out of the box" for most people! So create a safe space in which new ways of thinking, new bases for decisions, and new styles of creating can be discovered.

Intention and Stewardship

Intention is the first step in transforming energy into form. Your intention itself is an energy structure because thought is energy. In this first house, you actually deal with intention on two levels: the intention inherent in the potential—what wants to happen—and your intention for who you will be and what you commit to as the steward for what wants to happen. Therefore, this first house calls you to clarify the fundamental potential within your project and then commit to its manifestation.

The manifestation process begins with identifying a project, vision, dream, or goal you want to put on the Wheel. Next, you ask: What wants to happen here? What is the gift of this situation? What is this situation really trying to help me see? What is my desire truly about? What do I really want deep in the heart of my being? The manifestation process itself thus unfolds as an extended intuitive dialog with your project or vision, with its potential, and with the greater Consciousness. The dialog continues all the way around the Wheel until the manifestation is complete. Through it, you continue to follow the potential, committing to its full realization rather than a specific physical outcome. The ongoing dialog keeps the possibilities open for an outcome that is at least what you initially hoped for, and quite possibly much better.

Choose a project, vision, dream, or goal to put on the Wheel. With that project fully in mind, let the following exercise help you begin the dialog, first "talking" with your current conception of your project or vision, and then with its greatest potential.

Exercise 4: Discovering the Potential in Your Project

Begin by sitting comfortably, closing your eyes, and focusing your attention on your breath. Allow your breath to find its own natural, steady, even rhythm. Take time to settle into your Point of Stillness.

Bring your project or vision to mind as you currently conceive it and imagine it floating out in front of you. You may see it; you may feel it or hear it; you may simply sense its energy. However you perceive it is fine. Just notice it. Does it have a color, shape, or form? Does it have a sound? A texture? A fragrance or a taste? How would you describe your project energetically? What are its characteristics?

Now ask your project to show you or tell you its greatest potential. Ask it what really wants to happen. As you perceive the potential, how does it feel? How would you describe it? Does the potential have a color, shape, or form? A texture? A sound, fragrance, or taste?

Ask the potential what it needs from you—how you can be the best steward for it. Claim that potential and commit to it as the basis of your intention for this project.

Now float the project and its potential back into your body. Feel where it lands inside of you. Where does it live in you? Connect to that place in your body and know that place as your power spot for this project. Connect to that spot whenever you are engaged in any part of the manifestation process. This is where the greatest potential for your vision lives in your body. Then expand that potential to fill your whole body. Surrender to it and let it overtake you. Become an embodiment of the potential. Notice how your energy shifts. Do you feel different? In what way? What do you now know about your role as the steward for this project?

Take time to write in your journal about the potential you discovered and the commitment you made. Record your experience in this exercise.

The potential for your project will likely evolve as you journey around the Wheel. As the manifestation process unfolds, you and your situation or circumstance evolve, opening the door to even greater potential. The potential that you have as you step into the Wheel is based on where you are as you begin. As you grow and evolve through the manifestation process, this potential also evolves. The Manifestation Wheel facilitates evolution for you and for the potential.

Manifestation is a process of emergence. Calling forth and following the potential that emerges is key to the process. Your job is to act as a steward for the potential wanting to unfold. As you steward that potential and follow its energy, synchronicities occur as things start falling into place, leading to a synergy that propels the manifestation process forward. Even after you have created an action plan in the sixth house, your job is still to steward the potential and be guided by it. The act of stewardship must always take precedence over "sticking to the plan." The plan will and should evolve as you continue to understand what the potential is showing you. Your job is to be curious, to remain aware, and to keep in touch with how energy is flowing and potential rising.

Seeing into the Moment

Once you have made a commitment to your project and its potential, it is time to focus on the present and who you need to *be* in order to set the manifestation process in motion. In his 1996 television series, *Visionaries*, Bill Moyers said that people are visionaries "not because they see into the future, but because they see into the moment." In this first house of the Manifestation Wheel, you are called to see into each present moment and to be who you are called to be, to embody the potential of your vision in order to put yourself on a manifestation path that will lead to fulfillment and reward.

This "being" is beautifully expressed in the Japanese word *kokoro*, meaning literally "mind, heart, spirit" and having to do with perfecting your inner nature. In order to be great at anything, you must first perfect a way of being that is consistent with the greatness you desire. In mainstream Western culture, a person's way of being is given little importance. We mostly focus on knowledge, skills, techniques, and action. We ask: How do I do it? or What's the plan? Perhaps we would be better served to first ask: How should I "be" in order to accomplish my goal? Who are you as you enter the manifestation journey? And who do you need to be in order to see it through? Who is the person who would have and do whatever it is that your vision or project might be? What are the qualities of being necessary for successful manifestation of the greatest potential?

We all have dreams and goals. We feel called to a cause. We have deep desires. We usually think that we want to accomplish these things because of what we will get to do, the people we will get to be with, or how our lives or the world will be different in some tangible way. The truth, however, is that we want things because of who we will get to *be* and how we think we will *feel* once that thing is accomplished. If the project is a manifestation for others—like manifesting a community education center in a third-world country—the true driving force in the desire to manifest it is who the people of the community will grow to be through the offerings and programs of the center. It is the *being* and the *feeling* that we're really after. It's so easy to get caught up in specific outcomes, as if the physical manifestation of something in and of itself is the answer. The truth is that dreams and goals are important, not for what they are in realized form, but for what they represent on the energetic level and who they allow us to be.

Dreams and goals show you what is important to you or to the situation as energetic qualities and emotional feelings. The physical realization of the dream or the goal is simply the vehicle through which you get to be who you long to be, and to feel what you long to feel. It is the vehicle for creating the desired energetic field.

The physical realization of a dream, the accomplishment of a goal, or the completion of a project may create physical changes in your life, but the physical outcome is not what transforms you. It is the fundamental energetic essence that lies at the heart of the physical manifestation that leads to transformation.

Manifesting a new job is not what transforms your life. It is who you get to be within that new job, the new responsibilities you have and the ways in which they call you forth to be your best, as well as the new feelings of confidence and self-assuredness you gain through your new position that transforms you. The job itself is just the vehicle.

Developing a new service may give your business a higher profile for a while, but it is the focus on the energetic potential within that service and the resulting higher profile that truly transforms the business and brings lasting success at a new level. The higher profile that comes from the new service will only last as long as the life of the service. Potential, however, constantly evolves as you follow it and therefore is never-ending. Following the potential, your business can continue on an upward spiral of success.

Building the new community center is not what transforms the village. It's what happens in and around the center—the unfolding potential—that transforms individuals and the community and changes people's lives. When the sponsoring organization focuses on the potential for community impact and creating new opportunities for the people, the potential shows them what kind of building must be built and what the full program offered through the center needs to be. If they focus only on getting a new center built, they may not provide the necessary facilities for all that wants to happen through the center for the community.

Through the Manifestation Wheel, you will certainly manifest new situations and outcomes. Yet, more important, you will also grow into your greater potential. You will experience transformation as a result of the manifestation process. And that's ultimately what it's all about.

Transformation and Growth

Transformation and growth come from the inside out. Having or doing things will not make you the person you desire to be or take you to your greatest potential. You must live that potential on the inside in order for it to manifest on the outside.

Being the person you are called to be in your greatest potential opens doors for you to do and have everything that goes along with that way of being.

The Manifestation Wheel shows you how to keep your focus on the energy. It helps you let the potential guide you and let the greatest possible outcome reveal itself through the process. It calls you to embody the potential—to become it, to live it. That was the point of floating the potential into your body in the last exercise (see page 38). This is a critical step in the manifestation process. It is essential to embody the potential in order for the greatest alignment of energy to occur. The first house of the Manifestation Wheel calls you forth to *be* the potential you want to manifest, therefore becoming a magnet that attracts everything that is needed.

Once you begin attracting what is needed and have success at manifestation, you must understand how you got there if you want to continue that success. Then you repeat that pattern over and over. Conventional wisdom views that success path as a series of action steps. But actions are only one part of the equation. Even more important than your actions are your thoughts. It is critical that you recognize the thought patterns that led you to success and then make these thought patterns your habit. This takes discipline. Yet that discipline can lead to new freedom, which leads to greater command in whatever you are doing. It's like ballroom dancing. First you must have the discipline to learn the steps. Once you have learned them, your movements get freer and freer as you repeat them. In that freedom, you start creating new and wonderful variations on the steps. And you easily adapt to new partners as they come along. Soon, you have mastered a particular style of dance and made the performance uniquely yours. It's the same in yoga, martial arts, or any sport.

Mastering anything begins with discipline, which leads to freedom, which leads to command. In music, dance, acting, or sports, the highest forms of free improvisation are built on masterful command of a very solid technique and an awareness of everything that is going on around and within you. And that technique and awareness is only developed through disciplining your thought, intention, and choices.

So it is with the manifestation process. Mastery begins with tapping into the potential—what wants to happen—and then disciplining your thoughts to remain focused on that potential. That focus builds your technique, which leads to the freedom to create anything. And then you have command over your life and are a master at the technology of manifestation. You begin manifesting your life rather than having your life manifest you.

When someone is very good at manifesting, people often say they are just lucky. Deepak Chopra defines luck as "preparedness meeting opportunity." In the Introduction, I defined manifestation as a natural and even "somewhat predictable" product of your thoughts, beliefs, decisions, and actions. It is predictable because you set a clear intention, align your thoughts, beliefs, decisions, and actions, and are prepared when opportunity appears.

Opportunities are all around you. When you have an acute intuitive awareness of your surroundings and interactions, you notice them. Preparation plays a big part in that intuitive awareness. If you are prepared for opportunities and even expect them, you notice them when they appear. If you aren't prepared, opportunities pass you by. You may not always immediately recognize exactly what the opportunity means, what it will bring, or what uncharted waters you may enter, but you must be willing to take a chance and trust that the potential is unfolding toward the best possible outcome. That is your intention, after all, and the energy you have set in motion.

Choice and Focus

Part of being prepared for opportunities is making clear choices. In order to manifest a vision, you have to choose it. If you want to manifest a lot of money, you must first choose to have a lot of money. If you want to manifest more time with the important people in your life, you must first choose to have that time. If you want to help many people or to travel extensively, you must first choose that you are going to do it. Whatever you want in your life or feel called to do or have, you must first choose it. Again, alignment of energy is the deciding factor. The House of Intention is where it all begins. It is here that the Laws of Vibration and Attraction (see page 9) come into play. Put them to work for you! Make clear choices with definite intentions and discipline your thoughts to focus on the potential of your vision fully manifested.

When you focus on the potential of a vision or project, you focus on its essence—the seed within it that wants to develop in the best possible way. When you tap into your essence, you tap into your soul—the source of your true passion. Your soul is the life-giving force within you, the part of you that is one with the greater Consciousness, the source of your wisdom, creativity, intuition, and innovation. Your soul is a huge and expansive energy that wants to experience its greatness all the time. It will not invest in anything less. It thrives on learning, growth, and transformation.

Michelangelo said that the greatest danger for most of us is not that we aim too high and we miss, but that we aim too low and hit the mark. As you dive into your manifestation project, aim high. All too often, I see people who have a great vision, but then settle for just a little part of it. They talk a good game—they claim to aim high—but their thoughts and actions reveal that they are playing it safe. In reality, they are aiming low. They tell me of their great vision and describe the extraordinary life they could have or the incredible potential they see, but just when it is time to take action, they lower their sights and aim low. They never challenge themselves to stretch beyond who they are sure they can be and what they are sure they can do and have. Something inside them wants a guarantee that they won't be disappointed. Each time they aim low, their soul gets pushed aside and a little part of their spirit dies, resulting in chronic disappointment or dissatisfaction. They continually pass up opportunities to step up to their greatest potential. When you aim high, even if you don't hit the mark, your soul is still exhilarated. Your spirit is very much alive, because you are still growing.

You can only be disappointed when you are attached to a specific outcome. If you are committed to the process—the learning, discovery, growth, and transformation that can happen as you move toward your goal—and are willing to let the potential manifest in its greatest possible outcome, you are much more likely to experience reward and fulfillment in the process. Not every goal or dream will be fully realized as you originally imagined that it would be. However, as you take the manifestation journey, you will learn, stretch, grow, and be offered valuable opportunities. It will bring wondrous gifts that can lead you toward your vision, sometimes in astonishing ways.

So, aim high! Let go of attachment to an outcome and commit to the potential and the journey.

Before we leave the first house, declare your intention and make your personal commitments for the manifestation journey. The following exercise walks you through that process. Give it the time it needs. You are laying the foundation for the manifestation of your vision. Nothing stands for long without a solid foundation. So take your time. It will pay off in the long term.

Exercise 5: Stating Your Intention

It's now time to create your statements of intention and commitment. Begin by answering the following questions:

1. What is the project, goal, desire, or vision you are putting on the Wheel?

2. What is the greatest potential for this project or vision? What wants to happen?

3. What are the characteristics of the person that would fully manifest that potential?

4. Who do you commit to being through this manifestation process?

Now write your statement of intention. This should be as short as possible, yet still be clear. A few well-chosen words in a carefully crafted statement will carry much more power than a rambling statement with too many details. Find the words that will convey the full picture most clearly. This statement is for you only and therefore need only be clear to you. As long as the words are dynamic and powerful for you, that's all that matters. You may want to write a paragraph or more at first about your intention, and then condense it into the following form:

Project/Vision/Goal:

Potential:

Commitment:

When you start a new project that is important to you, you usually feel a lot excitement and enthusiasm—and sometimes some reluctance or apprehension. Your energy fuels your manifestation journey (you will learn more about this in the third house) and should be nurtured and protected. Some people in your circle will be very supportive of your endeavor and recognize its importance to you. Others, however, just may not get it. They may feel threatened in some way by your commitment to the project, or resentful of the importance you are giving it. All this is to say that you may not get support for your manifestation journey from everyone. Therefore, choose carefully what you share with others. When you speak with someone you know will support you and be excited for you, by all means share it. Their energy will help fuel the momentum. However, when you are not sure how someone will react, you may want to keep your thoughts and plans to yourself. Share your project only with those you know will offer the support and encouragement you need.

Just as your emotional environment is important to the accomplishment of your project, so is your physical environment. Spend time in places that are conducive to your sense of peace and growth, as well as places that offer whatever you may need in the manifestation of your vision.

The intention you have declared here is your intention as you understand it now. It may, and in fact often does, change or evolve as you go around the Wheel. That's one of the gifts of the Wheel—it helps you clarify what you truly want to manifest, as well as what illuminates your life or a particular time in your life. So if you feel your intention shifting as the potential unfolds through the houses of the Wheel, this is not unusual. Remember that you are stewarding potential, not specific outcomes. If the potential starts showing you something new, pay attention and respond accordingly.

Your manifestation journey has begun.

CHAPTER 4

House #2: Peace

Resolve conflicts, face fears, dissolve resistance.
Make peace with your intention, its
potential, and the possible outcomes.
Release the past.
Ensure that your project is in
harmony with your personal values.

The Manifestation Wheel calls you into self-exploration and discovery in order to align your thoughts, beliefs, choices, and actions. It calls you to know yourself at deep and profound levels. We have been talking about the importance of aligning thoughts, beliefs, and actions to the project and its potential, but there is another alignment—perhaps the most important—that we haven't yet mentioned. Your project, its potential, and all of the steps you take toward its manifestation must also be in harmony with your soul, your essence, your personal truth, the fundamental core of your being. When you think about your project or vision, your "gut feeling" must be good. If you have second thoughts, endure restless nights, or feel uneasy about any part of the project, something needs to be addressed.

While inner peace is critical to the manifestation process (we will devote a large portion of this chapter to reaching inner peace), the second house also asks you to look beyond your project to your relationships with family, friends, co-workers, other organizations, and the world at large. Certainly any conflict you have with the vision itself, its potential, or its process is going to stand in your way. Yet to give your greatest energy and focus to a manifestation project, you must be at peace in all areas of your life. Unresolved issues drain energy from your project. You will not be able to be fully present with the process if some part of you is focused on unresolved issues.

It is important to note that peace is not the absence of conflict, but rather your response to conflict. Challenge and conflict are part of life. Without them, there would be no growth. There would be nothing to "stir the pot" and bring you face to face with those parts of yourself that are ready for transformation. However, it is possible to have conflict and challenge around you and still be at peace deep in the heart of your being. You may not be able to choose every circumstance or situation in your life, or to change what is going on around you in every moment, but you can choose who you are within that circumstance or situation. You can choose to get caught up in the drama of what is going on around you, or you can rise above it, observe what is happening from a higher perspective, and then very consciously choose how and to what level you will be involved.

How do you do that? One way is to become aware of what Doc Childre, founder of the Institute of HeartMath and author of *The HeartMath Solution*, calls "high-heart" and "low-heart" energy. Both are rooted in feelings of love and care. Whether you are responding to a situation from a high-heart or low-heart perspective, you are probably there because you care about an issue, have a stake or interest in the outcome, or care deeply about someone involved. However, there is a big difference between high-heart and low-heart response. A low-heart response is rooted in feelings of sympathy, empathy, caretaking, and co-dependence. A high-heart response is rooted in feelings of compassion, unconditional love, and a higher perspective of what is going on.

When you are in low-heart energy, you automatically get pulled into the drama of the situation. Your reaction is driven by your personal need for things to be "okay," even though you may be telling yourself your primary concern is for the other people or the situation. When you are in high-heart energy, you can rise above the drama and your personal preferences and see more clearly what will support the greatest potential within the situation. You are the compassionate observer, able to step back, observe, and assess what is really going on, as opposed to the various "spins" being applied to the situation or stories being told by the players. You can then make clear choices about how, or even if, you will get involved. When you come from a high-heart perspective, you are in command of your emotions and actions. When you slip into a low-heart perspective, you move out of conscious response and into unconscious reaction.

The high-heart energy center is located in the upper-sternum area, midway between the center of your chest and the base of your neck. The low-heart center is located just below the center of your chest and just above your solar plexus. Many people can experience the difference between these two energies simply by taking in several breaths, first through one center, then through the other. Take a few moments for the following exercise and experience it for yourself.

Exercise 6: Using High-Heart/ Low-Heart Energy

Close your eyes and take deep and full breaths, filling your entire body with air. Continue this breathing and imagine the breath coming in through your low-heart center, down around the base of your sternum, between the center of your chest and your solar plexus.

After a few moments, shift your focus to imagine the breath coming in through your high-heart center in the upper-sternum area between the center of your chest and the base of your neck. Continue taking deep and full breaths. Just change where you imagine the air entering.

Notice how the low-heart and high-heart breaths feel different, and take time to record your impressions in your journal.

For most people, the high-heart breath feels more open and expansive, while breathing in through the low-heart center feels more restrictive. However, if you are accustomed to living in low-heart energy, the low-heart breath may feel more comfortable simply because it is your habit.

In the next few days, pay attention to when you are in conscious response and where you are in unconscious reaction— when you are approaching situations from a high-heart or low-heart perspective. This will heighten your awareness so that the next time you find yourself in a challenging situation, you can make clear choices. The moment you feel yourself being swept up into the drama, consciously breathe in through your high-heart center, filling your entire body with breath. Breathe all the way to your toes; then exhale through your solar plexus. Continue that breathing pattern for several minutes and you will feel yourself get calmer and feel your perspective shift.

This breathing technique can help you gain clarity and peace in the face of most challenges. I'm not claiming that this is a magical solution—"all you have to do is think nice thoughts and breathe into the magic spot and everything will be fine"— yet it can be a very powerful place to begin. Research at the

Institute of HeartMath in Boulder Creek, California, overwhelmingly confirms the value of this simple technique.

While making peace with outside challenges is important, inner peace presents the greater struggle for many. And there is nothing like clearly stating an intention and making serious commitments to the manifestation of that intention to call out your personal doubts, fears, and resistance. Stating intentions and making commitments are tantalizing bait for any part of you that isn't fully on board with your vision or doesn't believe it can happen. Although challenging in the moment, this is actually a good thing. Too often, we can't seem to make headway with something that we know really needs to happen, but we can't figure out what is getting in the way. Therefore, when doubts, fears, and resistance show themselves, they are gifts. They solve the mystery. We know the problem.

Ego and Soul

In chapter 1, we talked about soul and ego and how we are the bridge between the three-dimensional physical realm and the non-physical realm of Consciousness. A closer look at these two fundamental aspects of your being can shed more light on why inner conflicts arise and provide a means for resolving them.

Soul is your energetic essence. It functions within the more expansive intuitive mind that is a part of the greater Consciousness. It lives simultaneously in your physical body and in the non-physical realm. It was in existence before you were born; it was there within you when you were an infant, and through childhood and adolescence. It is within you now and for the rest of your life; it will continue to exist long after this life ends. It is the absolute truth of your being, the fundamental life-giving force within you. Soul energy is huge and expansive. It sees and understands the big picture of life and wants to know and experience its greatness. Its natural state is creation and manifestation, so it thrives on exploration, discovery, growth, and transformation.

Ego, on the other hand, is the aspect of your consciousness related to your physical body, your personality, your talents and skills—all the aspects of you that are connected to the physical world. Its primary role is to ensure your survival, so it thrives on safety, security, and guarantees. It functions only in the visible world, accessing only the rational mind or intellect, and the five outer senses. It has no awareness of anything beyond the obvious, three-dimensional world. Ego is often criticized for making "bad choices," having a narrow view, or being self-serving or arrogant. Yet when you consider that ego's primary function is to ensure your survival and well-being, you realize that, from its perspective, it's just doing its job. When ego puts up resistance, becomes self-centered, or tries to take over a situation, it's just doing whatever it perceives, from its limited perspective, is necessary to assure your survival and your ultimate success in the physical world.

Success from ego's perspective means being on top, staying in control, and having the most, so that nothing can threaten its power. It is rooted in a "survival of the fittest" mentality. From soul's perspective, on the other hand, success means reaching its potential for growth and transformation—a goal informed by love and understanding that we are all connected and serving the greater good.

Ego knows how the physical world works. It knows all about the rules and structures of daily life, because all of those rules and structures were designed by egos to create a space where we can all live together in relative accord. However, its knowledge is based solely on its direct experience—what it has observed and learned first-hand. As far as ego is concerned, if it has never experienced something, that thing does not exist or is not possible. Ego knows nothing of the vast, unseen, non-physical realms of Consciousness and will do whatever it takes to make sure that you stay in an environment that it deems predictable, safe, and secure.

Soul, on the other hand, is completely at home in the vastness of potential and possibility. It loves to explore new territory and the unknown. Yet the soul knows nothing of the rules and structures of daily life. Without ego as the physical component of being, your soul cannot accomplish anything in the physical realm. It may have big dreams, but on its own, it has no way to manifest them. Ego is the grounding force. Soul needs ego in order to create and accomplish in the physical world; ego needs soul for the "big-picture" view.

When you start talking about manifesting something new and making commitments for things you've never been or done before—at least not at this level—ego may revolt. Soul says: Yes! Let's go! Ego says: Are you crazy? Do you know what could happen? Don't you see the risk here? And then you are stuck. It's as if you are trying to drive a car with the emergency brake on and wondering why you aren't going anywhere. Ego's revolt can take the form of fear, doubt, resistance, or, in the most extreme cases, complete refusal to cooperate. It may not believe that what you say you will do is possible. It may not understand how it could happen. It may have past experience that tells it this is not safe.

Ego doesn't like the idea of potential and opening to the greatest possible outcome. That's too unpredictable. It wants to decide what the outcome will be and then make sure it happens. Ego leaves no room for error or chance. It wants guarantees, and will fight for control of every part of the process. Control, however, is not part of soul's vocabulary. Soul operates through synergy and synchronicity—energies that come together in extraordinary ways and lead to results that you probably couldn't have made happen, yet somehow don't surprise you. While soul fully understands and trusts the manifestation process, ego can't imagine how it works.

In the second house, ego and soul must be reconciled. Many teachings criticize ego for its poor behavior, implying that ego must be reconciled with soul. Some even advocate getting rid of ego altogether. However, reconciliation actually starts when soul embraces ego, loves it, and nurtures it, much as a good parent does a frightened child. Once ego realizes it is being cared for, that it is not being left to fend for itself, that it has an ally and support for this journey, and that it is not going to be compromised, it is more willing to come along. Over time and a number of manifestation projects, ego gets comfortable with the process of stewarding potential and is able to trust soul. The more you make manifestation a way of life, the more familiar ego becomes with the process and no longer feels threatened. Left on its own, ego reverts back to its old ways; in tandem with soul, it recognizes an ally, friend, and guide. In fact, the more comfortable ego becomes with the process, the more it actually surrenders to soul's leadership. When that happens, your most powerful inner partnership is born.

As ego surrenders to soul, it is transformed from a fear-based energy fighting for survival and pushing to maintain control, into the metaphorical hands and feet of your soul—as if soul were the captain of the ship and ego its willing and able crew. Through this transformation, your ego blossoms in its magnificence, realizing its full potential as a partner, not only in the powerful co-creation and manifestation of your life, but also in the realization of the gifts you have to share with the world. Through the soul-ego partnership, you experience the first level of co-creation. Co-creation must be present within you—soul and ego creating together—before you can co-create effectively with others and with Consciousness.

This may not be how you are accustomed to thinking about ego. However, if you want to become a master at manifesting the greatest potential of any situation or circumstance, and indeed living your greatest personal potential, you need the expansive vision of soul served by your powerful and magnificent ego. Living within this balance is not only an essential part of the manifestation journey; it is a critical component of inner peace.

Take time for the following exercise to initiate your soul-ego partnership.

Exercise 7: Initiating Your Soul-Ego Partnership

Close your eyes and focus on your breath, allowing it to find its own natural, steady, even flow. Don't try to manipulate your breath in any way—just let it find its own natural rhythm. Take your time.

Let go of any preconceived notion of what your experience should be and imagine your soul floating out in front of you. How does it show itself to you? Does it have a shape or a color? A texture? Does it have a sound? A fragrance or a taste? What does it feel like? How would you describe it energetically? What are the qualities of your soul?

Ask your soul to tell you its greatest strength. And then ask it how it feels about your manifestation project. What does it want to say to you about the project?

Imagine your soul floating into your body. Where does it settle in your body? How do you experience its presence within you? Take a moment to settle into that feeling and experience.

What is your overall feeling when you settle into your soul? Notice the quality of your breath: is it shallow or deep, tense or relaxed? How do you experience your energy when you are settled into your soul?

After a few moments in your soul, pause to capture any thoughts or feelings you may have in your journal.

Come back to your breath once again, taking the time you need to make sure it is even, steady, and relaxed. Then shift your awareness to your ego and imagine it floating out in front of you. Meet your ego as if for the first time. How does it show itself to you? Does it have a shape or a color? A texture? Does it have a sound? A fragrance or a taste? What does it feel like? How would you describe it energetically? What are the qualities of your ego?

Ask your ego to tell you its greatest strength—how it truly serves you the best. Then ask your ego how it feels about this manifestation project. Ask if there is anything that it needs in order to feel safe with this project. If it is clear that there is an issue to be addressed, take time to ask questions and have a conversation with your ego to explore the issue. Be curious, gentle, and compassionate, so that your ego has a safe space in which to express its needs.

Once the ego feels safe, ask it how it wants to express its strength and magnificence through this manifestation project.

Imagine your ego floating into your body and notice where it settles. How do you experience its presence within you? Take a moment to settle into that feeling and experience.

What is your overall feeling when you settle into your ego? Notice the quality of your breath: is it shallow or deep, tense or relaxed? How do you experience your energy when you are settled into your ego? Making no judgment of one being better than the other, just consider how this feeling is different from the feeling you have when you are settled into your soul.

Take a moment to capture your thoughts and feelings in your journal.

Now shift your awareness away from your ego for a bit and breathe into your soul once again. Allow your soul to expand to fill your entire body. Imagine that your body is hollow and that every bit of that hollow space is filled with your soul. Then let your ego expand to fill and serve your soul. Notice how your energy shifts. How does this feel? What do you experience? Ego in service of soul.

Now, just for a moment, go back to your soul and ego being separate, each in its own separate location in your body. First, go to your soul, separated from ego. Breathe into your soul and ground yourself there—in your soul only. Notice how this feels—how you experience soul alone without ego. Then leave your soul for a moment and ground yourself in ego alone. Notice how this feels—how you experience ego alone without soul.

Finally, return to soul awareness, expand your soul to fill your whole body, and expand the ego to fully inhabit and serve your soul—soul and ego together in partnership. What do you feel? How do you experience this?

Being totally honest with yourself, consider where you live most of the time? In ego alone? In soul alone? In some level of partnership? What are you learning from this experience? How has your sense of inner peace changed as soul and ego have become dynamic partners? Take time to record your experience in your journal.

Inner peace means that there is no place inside that you are afraid to go. It means accepting all aspects of self—the parts you like as well as the parts you don't. Fears, doubts, and resistance are usually expressions of ego. They are expressions of parts of you that need to be heard. When you give those parts a chance to voice their fears or concerns, when you honor those feelings and remain compassionate and loving toward them, most of their concerns can be laid to rest. When you ignore those fears and doubts, they fester in your subconscious mind. As time goes on, it takes increasing energy on your part to hold them at bay—to protect yourself from them. Those fears and doubts gain power over your life because they keep you from giving your full attention and energy to anything else. When you look them in the eye and engage them, however, you take that power back. You begin directing energy that was being spent on personal protection toward facing the fears, working through the doubts, and freeing yourself of the resistance. A friend of mine used to advise me to "invite the dragon to tea." Treat your fears and doubts as honored guests. Take out your best china, your finest tea, and those Belgian chocolates you've been saving for a special occasion. Sit in your soul as you learned to do in the last exercise and have a conversation with whatever the fear or resistance may be. You can even float the resistance out in front of you if that helps to facilitate the conversation. Use the exercise above as a model and adapt it to facilitate the conversations you need to have with yourself. Take your power back and feel your inner peace getting stronger.

Making Peace with Change

By its nature, manifestation brings change. If you are not comfortable with change, here is another area where you must make peace. When left on its own, ego will resist change because, from its perspective, change means risk and uncertainty. You may not be able to control everything that is happening. This makes ego very uncomfortable, while soul may not even notice. Soul understands that the potential has to find its way. Ego wants to tell it where to go. So the second house of the Wheel asks you to make peace with change—in fact, to welcome change. When you find yourself resisting change, have a conversation with the resistance just as we did in the exercise with soul and ego. Float the change out in front of you and have a dialog. Be curious and compassionate. Ask the change what gift it has for you and how you can best embrace it. Find the source of your discomfort and determine what it needs to embrace the change and move on.

When you meet resistance or roadblocks on the way to realizing your goals, it is easy to interpret them as signs that you are on the wrong track. It's true that there are times when the roadblocks and inner resistance are indeed messages to stop or to change direction. More often, however, they are there to help you strengthen your resolve. They give you opportunities to claim your vision even more fully, to commit to it on yet another level.

So how do you know the difference? In the moment, your intuition may be the only tool you have. And how do you know when to trust it? When the voice you are hearing or the impression you are receiving is speaking truth, there will be an expansive feeling accompanying the message. It may be subtle. You may notice that you are breathing a little easier. Your body may feel more open. You may experience a physical sense that this is right. If the voice or impression is not speaking truth, you may notice a tighter feeling in your body. Your breath may be shallower and more anxious. You may feel as if you are being confined in a small space. These are very general sensations, yet I find them to be fairly universal. Practice listening to and acting on your intuition when the stakes are not so high. As you do, pay attention to the sensations in your body and the messages your body is giving you. The more you practice and pay attention, the more you will learn your body's language and how it communicates. Our bodies give us signals all the time. We just have to learn to read and trust them.

Finding inner peace may involve allowing yourself to grieve a loss. The loss may be recent, or it may be a loss from the past with which you are still not fully at peace. Too often, we dive quickly back into our routines and responsibilities after a loss, not giving ourselves time to grieve properly. Or we obsess about our work and responsibilities to mask the pain. Allowing yourself to grieve and mourn a loss is part of the inner-peace journey of the second house.

Sometimes making peace involves letting go of a relationship, a habit, a belief, or a dream. Once you commit to letting go, however, there often seems to be a testing period—a time when it seems you are tempted in every possible way to go back into the relationship, to pick up the habit again, or to fall back into the former belief. These are all gifts—opportunities to keep choosing the new path. Every time you choose the new path, every time you affirm your commitment to what you want to manifest and to who you will be in the manifestation process, you get stronger.

Every experience, relationship, situation, and circumstance is a gift to be opened. Every sorrow, loss, challenge, or hurt contains within it at least one gift for every person involved. The gift may be the same for all; it may be different. It may be subtle; it may be profound. The more adept you become at finding these gifts—at looking for them automatically, certain that they are there—the easier it is to find peace in the midst of conflict or challenge. Seeking and finding the gifts gives you greater faith in the bigger picture—confidence that there is a reason for everything and that there are no coincidences. For the moment, you ride the wave, knowing that you are where you are for a reason, and in time, you will, hopefully, understand why.

There's a big difference between wishing for something and actually being ready to receive it. Making peace in the second house is a big step toward assuring that you are indeed ready to receive the outcome of your manifestation and all that it means for your life. And so we come to that ultimate question: Are you ready to manifest your vision and embrace all that this manifestation will mean? What will you do then? How will you respond? Being able to answer these questions in such a way that you feel at peace is vital to your manifestation process and a prerequisite for moving forward.

Below are some questions to consider as you complete your work, at least for now, in the second house. Notice that the last question returns you to the first house. The Manifestation Wheel is a circular process—it loops back on itself. At the end of each house, you must check back with each previous house to see if any of the discoveries and work of the current house require reconsiderations in the previous houses. In this way, you ensure continued alignment and synergy continues to build. Take your time with these questions. Ponder them. Then write about them in your journal.

- What is your "gut feeling" when you think about your manifestation project or vision? Are you at peace with it?

- Are you ready to accept the full manifestation of your vision? What will be different? How does that feel?

- Are you pursuing any part of the project because you think you "should" or because someone else thinks you should? If so, is this what really wants to happen?

- Do you have dreams or aspirations that remain unfulfilled and, in reality, may never be fulfilled? What must you release or reconcile in order to be free of the past and move forward with this project?

- Are there any hidden agendas here?

- What is your relationship to the world around you? Are there conflicts that need to be resolved before your goal or project can manifest? If so, how can you resolve them?

- What needs to shift in order for inner peace to be a way of life for you? What is one step you can take today?

- House #1 Check-in: After your work in the second house, what, if any, revisions need to be made to your intention and commitments of the first house? How do you see the potential of your project or vision differently?

On your first trip around the Manifestation Wheel, your work in the second house can seem overwhelming. Some people have a lot of work to do here. There is nothing greater than to be at peace in your life. Yet the importance of peace is rarely stressed in our culture. Instead, we focus on mechanisms to cope with the stress and discord. Coping is not a solution. It requires tremendous energy and focus just to keep the mechanism functioning. Why not spend that energy and focus on manifesting a new circumstance or situation or a new relationship to it? Spend your energy wisely. Find peace.

When you do the work of the second house, you not only work on your current manifestation project, you also lay the groundwork for many future projects. You bring your life into alignment with itself. Soul and ego become partners rather than combatants. Your thoughts, intentions, beliefs, choices, and actions come into harmony with your soul and what is most important to you. You bring your life into complete congruence. The payoff for doing this work is huge. It makes everything flow with greater ease and grace.

The House of Peace offers you the opportunity to stop coping and start resolving, healing, and releasing that which does not serve your project, and ultimately does not serve the greatest potential for your life. The House of Peace offers you freedom to aim high and hit the mark—the freedom required to be a master at manifestation and co-creation.

CHAPTER 5

House #3: Energy

Generate passion and energy.
Mastermind possible steps and goals.
Identify resources and alliances.
Create reality fields.

The focus of the first two houses is primarily on inner processes—setting intentions, making commitments, finding peace.
The third house begins the outer manifestation process. From
this point on, the Manifestation Wheel balances inner and outer
work, keeping you closely in tune with the energetic potential of
your project and the greater Consciousness, while identifying
and taking the necessary action steps in the physical world.

The third house of the Wheel is all about energy: generating energy and passion, assessing where the energy is strong
and where it is lacking, and learning how to work with energy
to manifest results. You begin your work in this house by
acknowledging energy as the power or driving force in your
manifestation process. Then you mastermind possible steps
that can be taken and goals that can be set. You identify
resources you will need and research possible alliances. You are

not yet creating an action plan, but you begin to discover and assemble components that will ultimately be a part of your plan. Informed by that work, you take another step in aligning your thoughts and emotions by creating reality fields. By the time you complete your work in this house, you will broadcast a stronger signal to the universe, and therefore be a stronger magnet to attract what is needed to manifest your vision.

The true source of power in the manifestation process is the energetic potential of your project. We often think that power lies in our actions—how we take charge of a situation, make decisions, keep control over every part of an operation, and ensure that "things happen." Power, in this sense, means power over something else, sometimes coercing others and forcing situations or results. The truth is that, when you tap into the energetic potential of your vision, you find a power far beyond what you can muster on your own. This potential can be a driving force that, when masterfully stewarded, inspires, guides, and directs you all the way through the manifestation process. Your job as steward is to tap into that potential, harness it, guard and protect it, and embody it. When you become the steward for your vision rather than the manufacturer or sole creator of a plan, you recognize that the power comes from the vision itself and your commitment to it. Knowing this, you can accomplish incredible things. It takes discipline and vigilance on your part to remain in that energy. The third house gives you tools to do this.

Begin your work in this house by assessing your level of excitement and passion for your project. Passion and excitement come from having a strong reason for manifesting your project. If your vision or project is just something that would be nice, you will probably not have a lot of passion about it. But if it's something that will significantly change or greatly enhance your life, you will find much more energy for manifesting it. You need to have a clear vision of how your life will be different once your vision is manifested. Take a few minutes to write in your journal about these questions:

- How will your life be different once your vision is manifested?

- In what ways will you feel different?

- What will you do differently?

- What will you have that you do not have now?

- Why do you want this? Why is it important to you?

- On a scale of one to ten, ten being the highest, what is your level of passion and excitement for this project?

Being clear about your answers to each of these questions builds your energy, enthusiasm, and motivation for manifesting your vision. Coming back to these questions can also help you when challenges arise. Asking them again can help put you back on track.

These questions also help streamline your focus and help you become more dedicated, disciplined, and efficient in your thoughts, choices, and actions. The more streamlined your focus, the greater the result you will achieve, often with less effort. When your life or organization lacks focus and structure, you spend energy. Time and space can fill up with things that aren't really important to you. If all your time, energy, and space are taken, there is no room for anything else. However, when you streamline your life or organization, more time, space, and energy are available for your manifestation project because they are all being used more efficiently.

The House of Energy requires that you consider what you must give up, at least temporarily, to accomplish your goals. Perhaps it is something tangible—a relationship, another project, a guaranteed income, or a responsibility that is demanding too much of your time. Or perhaps it is a thought pattern, belief, or habit. Perhaps it is something from the past. Or perhaps there is a risk that needs to be taken. Your project may require a significant investment of time and/or money. You must decide how much of each you are comfortable investing.

Consider the following questions. There are no right or wrong answers—only what feels right to you.

- Is there anything you must give up, even temporarily, to manifest your vision—activities, material things, habits, relationships, responsibilities, thoughts, or beliefs?

- Are you willing to do that?

- What are you willing to risk to manifest your vision? How much risk is acceptable? How much is too much?

- What do you risk by *not* manifesting your vision?

- Are you willing to invest time and money in your manifestation project? If so, how much?

The third house also introduces the practice of masterminding. Masterminding is similar to brainstorming, but offers more. When you brainstorm, you get lots of ideas out into the open, look at them from all angles, and analyze them to discern which are best. Masterminding takes this creative process a step further. In masterminding, you intentionally expand your mind into the intuitive realm and let things come to you. You may get intuitive "hits" in brainstorming, but you often don't know how they happened. When you mastermind, you intentionally open to another way of being, thinking, and exploring. You invite the greater Consciousness and the energetic potential of your vision or project to participate in the conversation.

In the first house, you experienced an intuitive conversation with your project to discover its potential and the personal commitments it requires. You can use a similar approach here. Whether you are working alone or in a group, take a moment first to go to your Point of Stillness, call the energy of your vision and its potential into the room, and begin a dialog. Below is a brief exercise to lead you through this process. Feel free to adapt it in any way to best meet your personal needs. If the exercise asks you to do something you don't think you know how to do, just ask yourself: What if I did know how? Imagine that you do know how and do it anyway. You may be amazed at how your intuitive mind kicks in when you are willing to give it a chance.

Exercise 8: Masterminding

Take a few moments to go to your Point of Stillness. Once you are settled, imagine the greatest potential of your project or vision floating out in front of you. Just have fun with this. You may "see" it, "feel" it, or "hear" it. Make no judgments or criticisms about what you perceive. Sense the level of energy, motivation, and passion present for the project. Is the energy and motivation high? Is there passion for this project? If yes, mastermind how best to harness that energy and passion. If no, mastermind how best to get the energy and motivation moving. There must be passion and personal motivation present to steward the greatest potential.

This part of your masterminding session may last a few minutes or, if ideas are starting to fly, it may last for quite a while. Just follow the energy, remaining aware of what wants to happen next and when it is time to move on.

To keep your masterminding session going, ask yourself open questions. Accept every idea, thought, or inspiration. Now is not the time to analyze things or think about whether something is a good idea or whether it will work. That blocks the energy. This process is pure inspiration and intuition. Make a note of every idea, even if you don't fully understand what you are thinking. Some questions to consider are:

- What goals can you consider as steps toward manifestation?

- What resources, including time, money, and expertise, must be attracted?

- What alliances may be helpful?

Follow the energy until it feels as if your masterminding session is over. Before you leave the session, take a moment to ask yourself about the experience. In what ways do you feel differently about the project and its manifestation? What do you know about the project that you didn't know before? How can you make the process work even better next time? And most important, notice how you did what you just did. Intuitive work is much simpler than we often make it out to be. Chances are, what you did was simply to get out of your own way intellectually and let it happen.

Many of the ideas that come out of this session may become a part of the action plan you create in the sixth house. Keep the notes from this session in a safe place so you can refer to them later.

Reality Fields

Once you have generated momentum, connected with your passion, and masterminded your manifestation project, it is time to create a reality field. A reality field is a physical or nonphysical space in which the energetic conditions or qualities are present for a particular reality to manifest. Reality fields are formed by your thoughts, emotions, and feelings. Together, they determine your vibrational frequency. When you embody the energetic potential of your project or vision, you take on its vibrational frequency.

The Law of Attraction tells us that like attracts like. When you create a reality field that has the same vibrational frequency as the potential that wants to manifest, you broadcast that vibrational frequency to Consciousness. (Remember the holographic metaphor of the eight-sided mirror?) As a result, you begin to attract everything that is needed. Synergy ignites and synchronicities start to occur.

In the modern Western world, we usually think of feelings and emotions as the same thing. Because we still operate primarily from a model that says that things are separate from one another, we usually don't acknowledge a connection between our feelings/emotions and our thoughts. However, the ancient cultures understood thoughts, emotions, and feelings as distinctly different yet totally interrelated aspects of being. According to this ancient wisdom, thought is simply your ability to focus and create direction. It is the organizing function of your imagination—your guidance system. Through it, you create a plan. Thought is a part of intellect, and therefore lives primarily in your head and upper-body energy centers.

Emotion is your belief, your passion, your fuel. It's what drives you. The ancient traditions speak of two fundamental emotions: love and fear. All emotion is rooted in one or the other of these two. Emotions rooted in love give you great passion, excitement, and productive energy. You feel expansive and optimistic about life. Emotions rooted in fear drain you of energy and cause you to pull in, to contract, and to feel anxious and apprehensive about life. Emotion lives primarily in the lower-body energy centers, from the solar plexus down.

When you have emotion without thought, you experience great energy and passion for making something happen, but lack direction and focus to do it. On the other hand, when you have thought without emotion, you experience clear direction and focus to accomplish something, but lack the energy or passion to do it.

Thought and emotion come together in the heart center to create feeling (see figure 3). Whatever you feel is actually your

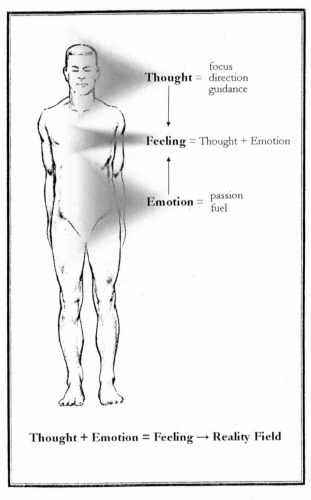

Figure 3. Anatomy of the reality field.

truth in that moment, and it is on that truth that you act. Your feeling creates your reality field.

You experience reality fields in a similar way as you experience feelings. In the manifestation process, you create a reality field that is very much like what you will experience once your vision has manifested. This field then creates an energy system that goes to work on your project. To say that you must "be" what you wish to manifest means that you must embody it and broadcast that vibrational frequency to Consciousness. The resulting field of energy becomes the reality you attract to yourself.

The Institute of HeartMath has done extensive research on the intelligence of the heart. Their studies show that the electromagnetic field of the heart is approximately 5000 times greater than the electromagnetic field of the brain.[5] That means that the heart's energetic field of awareness and influence is also 5000 times greater than that of the brain or intellect. Neither thought nor emotion alone is capable of generating enough energy to create a potent reality field. Heart-centered feeling, however, has a powerful impact on your life and your manifestation process.

Reality fields are essential components of manifestation technology. For the technology to work, you must have clear thought, focus, and intention around the potential you are manifesting, as well as an ability to listen intuitively to that potential and take direction from it. You must also have great passion for the potential and an absolute belief that its manifestation is possible. When thought and emotion are in alignment with one another, the result is a strong feeling, which in turn creates a potent reality field. That field attracts outcomes of similar vibrational frequency. When thought and emotion are not in alignment, the result is confused feelings that create a

[5] See Doc Childre and Howard Martin, *The HeartMath Solution* (San Francisco: HarperSanFrancisco, 1999), p. 33.

field of chaos and disorder, which can, in turn, make the outcome of your manifestation project confused and unsatisfying.

To manifest the greatest potential, your emotion must be rooted in love. When your fundamental emotion is love, your thought is fueled with positive energy and excitement. This creates a feeling of empowerment and confidence, leading to a reality field that attracts the outcomes you desire. When your fundamental emotion is fear, your thought is fueled with doubt, resistance, misgivings, and other emotions that hold you back and keep you trapped. This creates feelings of anxiety and apprehension and generates a reality field that attracts that which you most fear or resist. To manifest the greatest potential of your vision, therefore, it is imperative that you be aware of the fundamental emotion that is feeding your feeling and your reality field.

The following exercise can help you clarify your thoughts, emotions, and feelings so that you are fully aware of the reality field you are creating for your project.

Exercise 9: Identifying Thought, Emotion, and Feeling

Take a moment to settle into your Point of Stillness. Bring your project or vision to mind. Go to your intellect and focus all of your awareness on what you "think" about this project. Make no judgment on what you discover. Just observe. What are your thoughts?

Stay with your vision or project, leave your intellect, and drop down into your body. What emotions are you experiencing? Is your emotion fundamentally based in love or fear? Just observe. Make no judgment.

Now go to your heart center where thought and emotion come together to create feeling. What is your feeling about your project?

What is the reality field you are creating right now? Does it serve you? Does it hold the energetic conditions (aligned thought and emotion) that will support the unfolding of your project's potential?

If your answer is yes, continue to reinforce the thoughts, emotions, and resulting feelings that are creating that field. If your answer is no, consider what reality field would support that potential? What needs to shift in your thought to create and support that field? What needs to shift in your emotion? What is the feeling you need to create?

Take time before moving on to address these questions and make sure that you are creating the reality field that will serve both you and your project the most effectively. Take time to write about this in your journal.

Everything exists in a field of energy. Any particular energy field is created and influenced by the vibrational frequency of the person, object, or idea that is at its center. The more powerful the focus, intensity, and commitment of the person, object, or idea, the stronger, more dynamic, and powerful the energy field will be. The more dynamic and powerful the energy field is, the greater influence it will have on anything else that enters into that field. In any situation, the strongest vibrational frequency will prevail.

Energy does not recognize title, hierarchy, or rank; it exists aside from structure. It offers equal opportunity for creation and manifestation to all. The person, group, belief, or idea that has the greatest focus, the most intense vibration, and the highest vibrational frequency holds the energetic power. Whatever that belief or idea is, that person or group holding it will be the driving force in the situation. In manifestation, this means that the stronger your focus and intention, and the more complete your embodiment of the potential, the more likely you are to manifest your vision.

You have probably been a part of a group in which a single member, often not the official leader, seemed to hold the power. This person may have had a very strong personality and been very vocal about their feelings and opinions. Behind that personality and those opinions were very focused thoughts and emotions. Therefore, regardless of the opinions or feelings of others, whatever that person wanted was probably what happened. On the other hand, you've probably been in a group where a particular person was generally very quiet, yet their presence in the room was very powerful. On those occasions when they did speak, everyone listened with close attention because they knew something important was being said— something that would need to be considered seriously. Pay attention to energy in groups and how individuals impact group decisions and actions. Learn to monitor the energy and know what needs to happen next.

Monitoring energy is an important skill in manifestation. Pay attention to where the most powerful and influential energy is at all times. Is your manifestation process truly being driven by the potential, or by something else? If things are moving in the direction you understand to be the greatest potential, let the driving force continue. If not, what needs to shift within you to focus the energy, raise the vibrational frequency, and increase its intensity?

All possibilities for the future are present in Consciousness. When you create a reality field, you actually create the energetic conditions that will attract the future outcome you desire, that will encourage the potential to manifest into physical form. You actively steward the potential of your project across the bridge from the unseen world to the seen, from idea to reality.

Your individual choices and the reality field you choose to create determine which of the possibilities you actually manifest.

It's very important to recognize that, in creating a reality field, you are not creating a specific reality. You must focus, rather, on creating a field of energy that vibrates at the same frequency as the outcome in order to best serve the emerging potential. In *The Isaiah Effect*, Gregg Braden writes, "Rather than *creating* our reality, it may be more accurate to say that we create the conditions into which we *attract future outcomes*, already established, into the focus of the present."[6] That is what creating reality fields is all about—creating a field of energy in which all the conditions are present for a particular outcome to manifest. When you fully embody the energetic potential of your vision, the holographic principle kicks in and reflects it out into Consciousness. Reality fields are one of the most powerful ways that you can steward potential.

Reality fields are a fact of life. You are constantly creating them whether you are aware of them or not. They travel with you wherever you go. In the Introduction, I pointed out that you are constantly manifesting your own life. This is true because your thoughts and emotions are constantly coming together to create reality fields that attract circumstances, events, experiences, and relationships that match their vibrational frequency. When you steward the potential for your vision or project, you consciously choose the reality field in which you live. You have to discipline your thoughts and emotions to create the feelings that will sustain that field. When you first create a new reality field for your vision, it may not yet be your "default" or habitual way of life. You must be vigilant and constantly reinforce the new field until it becomes your default way of life. If the field is not consistent and sustained, you will not consistently attract what is needed. When you

6 Gregg Braden, *The Isaiah Effect* (New York: Three Rivers Press, 2000), p. 24.

have become a master at creating and sustaining reality fields, manifesting what you desire becomes a way of life. You are guided intuitively through each choice, decision, or action.

Energy Leaks

Even when you have become an expert at creating and sustaining reality fields, the energy may slip from time to time, or things may not seem to go as you feel they should. This may be a sign that something in your thoughts and emotions is not in alignment, that there is an "energy leak" in the system.

When you have a leaky pipe somewhere in the plumbing of your house, the water pressure drops through the whole system. The leak actually holds the power, because it causes the water pressure to drop everywhere. When you hold even the tiniest doubt, fear, or resistance about manifesting your vision, you create an energy leak in your project. If something is not in complete alignment between your thoughts, emotions, and vision, it can create a leak in the reality field that drains energy and makes the field less potent. Ninety-nine percent of you may be supporting the vibrational frequency of the new field, but the one percent of you that isn't holds the power. Therefore, it is important to fix the leaks when you discover them so that you reclaim the power.

There are several possible causes of energy leaks. First, check to see if both thought and emotion are fully engaged. If your thought has no emotion behind it or your emotion has no thought directing it, there won't be enough energy to support a strong reality field. If thought and emotion are both engaged, then check to see if they are in alignment with one another, supporting the feeling that will create the appropriate field. Hidden agendas can also create serious energy drains, because they support a lack of honesty and integrity in intention. There are hidden commitments behind those agendas that, if strong enough, can block the potential from manifesting. Energy leaks can also occur when you operate from someone else's reality field, or from the field of an idea or principle that is not in harmony with your soul.

The following exercise can help you identify the source of any leaks that may exist in your current reality field. It can also help you strengthen that field by taking a quick visit to the future, giving you a preview of what is to come in the fourth house, Guidance.

Exercise 10: Strengthening Your Reality Field

This exercise is best done in an open indoor or outdoor space where you can move freely. Begin by taking a few moments to settle into your Point of Stillness. Then stand in a spot you choose to represent the present time.

Bring your project or vision to mind. First, focus your attention only on your thoughts about your project. Scan your thoughts for energy leaks—any thought that may be getting in your way. Just observe them. Don't get caught up in them or make any judgment about them. You are simply gathering information.

Drop down into your lower body and focus your awareness solely on your emotions. What are your beliefs about this project? Is the fundamental emotion love or fear? Scan your emotions for energy leaks—any emotion that may be getting in your way. Again, make no judgment; just observe.

Move to your heart center. What is the feeling there? How would you describe the reality field being created in this moment?

Now move to stand in a different space that you choose to represent a year after your project has been completed or your vision manifested. Take time to imagine it. What has happened? How does it feel? Embody that energy. Pay attention to its qualities. What reality field is present? Describe it. How does it feel?

While standing in this new reality field, focus your awareness solely on your thought. What are your thoughts now that your vision is fully manifested, your project complete?

Once you are clear about your thought, drop down into your body, to your emotion. What do you experience a year after the vision has manifested?

Remain firmly grounded in these thoughts and emotions and in this new reality field, and move back to the spot that represents the present, bringing the reality field of the future with you.

As you stand in the present moment in the new reality field, explore your thoughts once again. How have they shifted? Is there anything in your thought that is still getting in the way of you reaching the future you experienced? Again, just observe.

Now drop down into your body and explore your emotion. What has shifted here? Is there anything in your emotion that is still getting in the way of you reaching the future you experienced? Just observe.

What is your feeling now? How would you describe your reality field?

If any blocks in thought or emotion are still present, take them to the future spot where the project has been completed or the vision has been manifested for a year. What do you know about those thoughts or emotions from this reality field? Once the blocks are resolved, move back to the present, taking the new reality field with you.

Take time to check in with thought and emotion once more. Continue this process of dialog and resolution between the future and the present until you are able to stand fully in the reality of the future, even in your present time. Then memorize that feeling.

Take time to record your experience in your journal.

It is important to check the energy status of your reality field periodically. From time to time, pause to ask: Is this reality field serving the greatest potential of my project? Is the energy moving toward manifestation? Remember that, as your project develops, its potential evolves. You have to "tend" your reality field just as you would a garden—pulling weeds, fertilizing, and watering. Energy leaks in reality fields must be discovered and repaired so that the strongest and most potent field can be sustained.

I'm often asked how creating a reality field is different from traditional prayer. Prayer is usually a request to God for something. When you ask for something, you, in effect, reinforce the fact that you do not have it or it has not yet happened. You reinforce the separation between you and what you desire. Depending on your approach, prayer can even be disempowering if you simply ask for something to be taken care of without claiming your personal role or responsibility in its manifestation. There is no co-creative engagement.

Creating reality fields, on the other hand, involves fully claiming your role in the active manifestation of your vision. You shift your vibrational frequency to a new level. You step into powerful co-creation with the greatest potential held within your vision and with Consciousness instead of waiting for an outside force—God or something else—to take care of it. If prayer is a part of your spiritual practice, let your prayer be an expression of gratitude for the potential having manifested. Pray for the reality that you desire, not the hope that it will come.

A reality field is not an action plan. It is a vibrational frequency that you embody. As you live in this field you have created for your project and work through the next two houses, an action plan will begin to emerge. In the sixth house, you will formalize that plan and begin to implement it.

Through your work in this House of Energy, you increase momentum, claim responsibility, mastermind ideas, and intentionally create a reality field. The energy, passion, and momentum for your vision or project should be strong now. If it isn't, consider whether your chosen project is indeed something for you to manifest. Again, make no judgment. Just be honest with yourself.

Perhaps you need to return to the first house to revise your intention, or to the second house to find a new level of peace. Let these closing questions help you recognize where you are in the manifestation process:

- Do you possess true passion and excitement for this vision? If not, what would call it forth? What still needs to shift? How can you do that?

- What needs to happen to continue to build a sense of momentum and energy focus toward this vision?

- What does your current reality field feel like? Does it fully serve the manifestation of this project?

- House #1 Check-in: Does your work in the third house reinforce your intention and commitments, or cause you to question them? Is there anything that needs to shift in your intention and commitments? If so, what?

- House #2 Check-in: Does your work in the third house in any way compromise your sense of peace about the manifestation of your vision? Do you still feel at peace with all that is unfolding? If not, what needs to shift?

CHAPTER 6

House #4: Guidance

Engage your intuitive mind.
Pierce the veil of time and space.
Remember the future.

The Manifestation Wheel engages your intuitive mind at every step of the journey. Through intuitive processes in the first three houses, you identify the greatest potential of your project, have conversations with your soul and ego, mastermind possibilities, and experience reality fields. The fourth house, Guidance, engages your intuitive mind to pierce the veil of time and space and remember the future. By visiting the future, you learn more about your project, explore possible outcomes through which your vision's potential can actually manifest into form, and develop a sense of how it will happen. This information gives you greater clarity about how your project will unfold. It also informs the action plan you design and implement in the sixth house.

As you work with the future in this house, it is important that you do not forecast or predict the future from your current point of reference. Instead, you use your intuitive mind to visit the future and explore it as if it were the present. You ask the future to show you what is possible as an outcome of your project, trusting that, since you are stewarding potential and inviting the best possible outcome to manifest, the future may offer more than you imagined. The fourth house asks you to suspend your pre-conceived notion of what it will be like when your vision is manifested, let go of expectations, and allow yourself to be shown how the potential wants to unfold.

Albert Einstein once said: "Time is not at all what it seems. It does not flow in only one direction, and the future exists simultaneously with the past."[7] In the realm of Consciousness and the quantum field, there is no linear time and space as we know it. Everything happens at the same time. Nor do things happen in specific locations; they happen as ideas that are everywhere at once. The Law of Mentalism states that everything exists within Consciousness and Consciousness exists within everything. Our minds exist within Consciousness and, at the same time, Consciousness exists within our minds. Our minds are, in fact, holographic images of Consciousness. In our linear-time, three-dimensional world, we accept the ability to remember the past without question. The non-linear, pure-energy world of Consciousness and the quantum field invites us to accept that we can remember the future as well. If working with energy and intuition is new to you, this may be a mind-bending concept—but stay with me!

If the past, present, and future all exist at the same time in Consciousness and the quantum field, why shouldn't you be able to remember the future as well as the past? And if events exist in those realms as energy and ideas rather than in three-dimensional form in a specific location, then why shouldn't the energy or idea be as available to you now as it will be a year from now or even fifty years from now?

---

[7] As quoted by Gregg Braden in *The Isaiah Effect*, (New York: Three Rivers Press, 2000), p. 83.

Scientists don't really know what energy is. They only know that it exists, it can be measured, and it can be organized to form ideas and matter. Patterns of energy go together to form information. Walter Schempp, a mathematics professor at the University of Siegen in Germany, discovered that the quantum field is a vast memory store. This discovery led him to the theory that memory does not reside in the brain, but rather in the quantum field. From that discovery, scientists and theorists went on to propose that the brain is merely a retrieval mechanism that recovers information from the quantum field where it is actually stored. This explains how one thought or stimulus can be the catalyst for an explosion of memories, inspiration, ideas, and comprehension. It also explains instant memory recall, which lets you locate a specific memory or bit of information without sorting through a vast "filing system" of memories. It offers a possible explanation for what Eastern mystical traditions speak of as the Akashic Records, a massive virtual library of sorts containing all the knowledge, wisdom, and information about all that has ever been, is now, and will ever be. And most important for the technology of manifestation, it explains how it is possible to remember the future. Your brain simply taps into the quantum field via the web of Consciousness, where all time and space co-exist, and retrieves the information you need.

Granted, your intuitive skills must be well developed to tap into the quantum field and gather specific information about other times and events. However, developing these skills is not difficult. You can enhance your ability to access that information simply by developing your intuitive mind. It just takes focus, commitment, discipline, and, most important, a willingness to expand beyond your rational thought process into a world that your rational mind may not be able to explain. Developing your intuitive skills and being able to remember the future requires that you suspend judgment about what you can and cannot do, what is and is not possible, and do it anyway. The more you practice, the more skilled you become. The processes of the fourth house give you a structure for remembering the future.

Since everything exists in Consciousness and the quantum field as potential rather than form, there are many possibilities for how that potential can actually manifest. (Remember the definitions of potential, possibility, and outcome on page 32.) When you first ask the question "What wants to happen here?" you are looking for the greatest potential or energetic essence that can unfold. As you steward that potential across the bridge from the unseen to the seen world, the potential shows you possible outcomes—various forms through which the potential can manifest. All of those possibilities exist in the realm of Consciousness. When you remember the future, in a sense, you actually retrieve one possibility of how things may turn out. When you remember another outcome, you retrieve another possibility. In Consciousness, all of the outcomes exist simultaneously. The outcome that actually manifests in your three-dimensional linear-time world is a product of all the conditions present and all the choices made.

The Potential Expressway

Imagine an expressway with at least five or six lanes in each direction. Imagine that each lane ultimately leads to a different destination. The expressway represents potential; the individual lanes represent possibilities. The lanes will ultimately diverge and go to different destinations, but here, where all the lanes are still together, the expressway (potential) can take you to any of those destinations (possibilities). Let's make this a magical expressway and imagine that one lane takes you to New York, another to Buenos Aires, and others to Copenhagen, Tokyo, Cairo, and Sydney.

When you enter the highway, all the lanes are running side by side. At this point, you can switch back and forth between lanes without committing to a specific destination, because all of the lanes are traveling together. However, after a few miles, the lanes begin to diverge and head toward their specific destinations. There is no mystery as to where each lane will take you. They are clearly marked, so you know as you choose a particular lane where you will end up. If you aren't sure which destination is the right one for you, you can travel to each one to check them out. You may choose to travel in the New York lane for a while to see what that journey is like, or even go all the way to New York to see how that feels. If New York is not to your liking, you can return to your starting place on the expressway and try another lane and destination. You can try them all before you make a final choice of a city in which you will ultimately settle.

So it is with the potential for your project. In the first house of the Wheel, you named your project and then identified the greatest potential for that project. In effect, you got on the Potential Expressway. Because you focused on the greatest potential rather than on a specific outcome, you were free to travel in any lane with the confidence that any lane on this particular highway would ultimately lead to full manifestation of that potential. In the second house, you got comfortable driving on this expressway, resolving any conflicts or doubts you had about the trip. In the third house, you did some shopping to procure all the supplies you needed for the journey, still not knowing exactly where you were going, just knowing that, whatever the outcome, it would fulfill the greatest potential of your vision.

Now in the fourth house, the expressway lanes begin to diverge. You see clear signs that name the possible outcomes of your manifestation project and indicate which lanes will lead you to which possibilities. Now you get to choose which lane you will follow, which possibility deserves your focus and energy for the rest of your journey.

Since the lanes have not yet diverged and are still side by side, the fourth house gives you the opportunity to explore each lane, each outcome, and see how it feels. You can take a virtual trip to each outcome, take note of how it feels intuitively, and make choices about which possible outcome feels like the right one.

The following exercise adapts this metaphor to help you discover and identify specific outcomes that are possible for your manifestation project. You may want to read through the entire exercise once before actually doing it.

Exercise 11: Traveling the Potential Expressway

This exercise is best done in an open indoor or outdoor space where you can move freely. Choose a spot to represent the present time in your life and stand there. Before you begin, close your eyes and reinforce your reality field and your embodiment of your project and its greatest potential.

Let go of any pre-conceived ideas or expectations about what you should experience or discover. With your eyes still closed, imagine yourself on the Potential Expressway, a magical highway whose lanes can take you anywhere in time or space. The entire expressway is reserved for you right now; there is no one else on it except you and those who may be a part of your future. So take your time; don't worry about holding up traffic.

You can travel this expressway using any mode of transportation. You can drive a sports car or ride in the back of a limousine; you can travel in a speedboat or yacht, on a bicycle or in a private jet; you can walk or even hitchhike. Have fun with this and let your intuition show you the best vehicle for your journey.

As you travel down the expressway, the lanes begin to diverge, each going in a different direction. You may see signs telling you where the different lanes are going, or you may not. Don't worry. Trust that you will recognize each possible outcome when you arrive there. Choose a lane to travel, open your eyes, and move to a spot that you choose to represent your first possible outcome. Standing in the energy of this outcome, consider the following questions:

- What is this outcome? Describe it.

- Tune in to the energy of this possibility. How does it feel?

- Who do you get to be here?

- What are the benefits of this particular outcome?

- What is the date now that your project is complete and this outcome is realized?

- Was the journey to this outcome easy or challenging?

- Is there anything about this outcome that you don't like?

- On a scale of one to ten, with ten being the best, how would you rate this outcome?

Stay with your feeling and intuition; resist the temptation to figure things out or analyze them. Just take what comes.

Now, go back to your starting place, close your eyes, and imagine yourself once again on the Potential Expressway with all of the lanes running side by side. Choose another lane and follow it as it diverges from the others and heads to its specific outcome. You may see a sign telling you where you are headed; you may not. Don't worry. When you are ready, open your eyes and move to a different spot that you choose to represent this possible outcome. Consider the questions above for this outcome.

Repeat this process until you have visited each of the possible outcomes, answered the questions there, and felt the energy of each outcome. Once you have visited each outcome, go back to your starting place and reflect on all the possible outcomes. Which one got the highest rating? Which one does your intuition tell you is the one to choose because it just feels right? You may want to revisit all of the outcomes and their spots again briefly. Go stand in each one for a moment and compare how they feel.

Choose the outcome you want to focus on as you continue in the manifestation process, and then go back to the spot that represents that outcome. Breathe in the vibrational frequency of the outcome. Feel its energy and embody it. What is the realty field that is automatically created when you embody that energy? Memorize it. Lock in that feeling. In exercise 15, we will come back here to take the next step in working with the future.

You've just learned a great tool for exploring the future, checking out possibilities, and making choices. While you are still in the energy of the outcome you chose, let's see what you can learn about the steps you can take to bring that future to the present.

Exercise 12: Embodying the Future and Reinforcing the Reality Field

Stand with enough space around you to take a step forward. Close your eyes and settle into your Point of Stillness. Imagine in front of you a movie of some point in the future when your project or vision is fully manifested. Look into the picture and feel its energy. Notice who is around you. Notice what sounds you hear. How would you describe yourself in that picture? Does what you perceive of the future feel good or right to you? Is it what you want? If not, what needs to change in your intention? What would make it feel right to you?

When what you see and feel is what you want, step into the movie and begin living it. Embody the energy and vibrational frequency. Check to make sure that everything feels right to you. Describe your reality field. Is it the same as the reality field you created in the third house, or is it different? If different, which of the two fields will best serve the manifestation of your vision?

As you embody the energy of your vision now fully manifested, what do you know about the focus of your thought and action for the next six months? What must the focus of your thought and action be for the next month? The next week? For the rest of today?

Take time to write about this experience in your journal. Make note of the components you discover. They may become a part of the action plan you create in the sixth house.

Now you have been to the future and seen at least one and perhaps a number of possible outcomes for your project. You have chosen the one that feels the best to you and let it show you more about the road ahead. It is important that, even though you have chosen a more specific outcome to manifest, you still listen to and follow the underlying potential that is manifesting through that outcome, not the outcome itself. Having a specific outcome as your focus from this point on is necessary for creating a clear action plan and implementing it. You now know specifically what you are manifesting. However, you remain committed to the potential as it unfolds through that outcome. The outcome is just a vehicle for the realization of the potential. If you focus on the outcome, you can easily fall back into making something specific happen rather than following the potential and continuing to align energy. The potential must still be the driving force for the optimal result.

Occasionally when visiting the future, you may sense a possibility that is disturbing or even frightening. Remember that any outcome you see is just one of many possibilities. In the realm of potential, nothing is set in stone. Everything is still a possibility. Nothing has come into form. Therefore, if you perceive something about the future that doesn't feel good to you, consider what you can shift on the path toward that event or circumstance to create something different. For example, if you sense a serious illness in your future, what can you shift now to avoid the illness? You may take proactive steps to change your diet, get more exercise, or learn about other ways of strengthening your body and immune system. Having seen the possibility, you have a chance to make different choices *now* so that you create a different future. You have the power to change lanes.

Once aware of a challenging possibility in your future, you can ask what that challenge can help you learn, experience, or understand. Then *you can choose now* how you want to learn that lesson or gain that understanding, rather than coping with it in the challenging form you sensed. For example, you may sense a serious financial challenge ahead. When you ask why you manifested that particular challenge in your future, the intuitive response may be that you had to learn to make clear financial choices and understand the power of money as energy. You can choose to make that shift now and quite possibly avoid facing the challenge later. The more you accept the gift or learn the lesson now, the less severe the future challenge needs to be. Since you've taken away the need for it, there is a good chance it will never happen.

If the challenge ahead feels inevitable, you can choose who you will be in the face of that challenge, how you will accept it and work with it from the moment it appears. This gives you the opportunity to move through the challenge with relative ease and grace. When you are prepared, you can approach almost anything from a sure place of stillness and clarity.

Finally, if a challenge does come, look for the gift. What is the challenge offering you? You have attracted it into your life for a reason. Make the most of it. Get all you can from it. And then move forward. The more self-aware you are and the more developed your intuition, the more you can perceive what is ahead and remain balanced, calm, and at peace as you walk the path.

The Point of Stillness meditation is a great place to start to prepare yourself to meet challenges when they arise. In the second and third houses, you learned other tools for working through challenges and conflicts, and for creating reality fields. Use those tools. Go back to those houses and work through the challenge that has come up. Then resume your journey from a place of greater clarity and peace.

When we talk about time in the manifestation process, we must also talk about patience and faith. Confucius said: "Great things have no fear of time." If you are living in a reality field that serves your vision, and if your thoughts, intention, beliefs, choices, and actions are in alignment with the potential of your vision and with your soul, and if you are open to allowing the potential to manifest in the best possible way, then things will happen, energy will move. Be patient and let things unfold in their own time. Trust that things are moving forward.

Sometimes, however, patience can be an excuse not to move forward. You may be telling yourself that you are just being patient and waiting for things to unfold when the fact is that you are really avoiding moving forward. Recognize the difference for yourself. You will know intuitively which is the case for you. True patience feels peaceful and still. Using patience as an excuse ultimately creates inner conflict and becomes an energy leak because, at some level, you know that you are avoiding accomplishing your goal. You know that you are not being the true steward that your project needs to manifest into form.

In this fourth house, you receive guidance from the future that can inform your manifestation process. You expand into your intuitive mind, explore various possibilities of how the greatest potential of your vision may manifest, and choose a specific outcome for your focus as you continue in the manifestation journey. As you wrap up your work in the fourth house, take time to consider the following questions:

- What more do you now know about your project, its potential and possibilities, and the road ahead?

- Now that you have visited the future, are there thought patterns, habits, or beliefs that need to shift to best facilitate the manifestation of your vision? If so, what are they and how can you make the shifts?

- Are you being patient with regard to your project? Is there a good balance? Do you need to be more patient? Are you resisting moving forward?

- House #1 Check-in: How has your understanding of your project or vision shifted now that you have visited the future? Do your intentions or commitments need revision?

- House #2 Check-in: Is your sense of peace compromised in any way now that you have visited the future? If so, what needs to shift?

- House #3 Check-in: Did visiting the future create more or less enthusiasm and motivation for your project? If less, what needs to shift?

CHAPTER 7

House #5: Empowerment

Call forth the best from everyone involved in the project.
Consider your project within the context of community.
Assess and step into the leadership required for your project.

To empower someone is to give them power or authority in a particular realm. You could also say that to empower an individual or a group is to call forth the power from within them—to call forth their strengths, talents, skills, and abilities, as well as their knowledge and wisdom. The fifth house of the Manifestation Wheel asks you to look at how your vision or project calls forth the best from you and from everyone who will be touched by it. It asks you to examine whether or not your project is serving you and all who are involved. It asks you to make sure that the message your project conveys to the world is in harmony with its potential.

There is an old Irish proverb that says: It is in the shelter of each other that the people live. The fifth house of the Wheel asks you to consider your project within the context of your larger community, the impact it will have on others, and how it will serve the greater good. It asks you to assess your relationships and be clear about which relationships serve you, support you, and empower you to manifest your vision. It asks you to determine which relationships encourage you to live your greatest potential and which do not. It asks you to consider how your project can actually improve relationships by taking them to the next level of nurture and support. And it asks you to look at nurture within the context of potential, instead of just as a means to keep a person or a group comfortable.

Finally, the fifth house explores your relationship to leadership, especially as it relates to your project. Does the project itself call you forth to leadership and, if so, on what level: personal, familial, organizational, or in larger arenas such as business, community service, or politics?

Begin your work in the House of Empowerment by looking at nurture and support as they relate to your project and to your life in general. To nurture someone or something means to take care of it, protect it, provide for it, and support it to fulfill its greatest potential. The fifth house calls you to nurture yourself and others involved in your project. And it calls you to allow yourself to be nurtured by others and by the project itself. Nurturing yourself means tapping into the greatest potential available to you in various aspects of your life and letting that potential guide you in your development.

Nurture does not necessarily mean keeping yourself comfortable. In a particular situation, nurture may mean challenging yourself, just as a mother bird pushes her babies out of the nest to force them to fly. Nurture of others means fostering their growth in their path of development—helping them be all they can be in their own potential, power, and strength, not in what or who you want them to be or think they should be. Nurture is not a license for manipulation of self or others. It is a means of empowering others to be all they can be. As steward for your vision, part of your job is to nurture your project's greatest potential and the outcome you chose in the fourth house, and to nurture the greatest potential of everyone directly or indirectly involved in its manifestation. Your direction and guidance for that nurture comes from intuitively listening to the potential itself, to your soul, and to the souls of those involved. Through that awareness, you find the best ways to call forth the greatest power, skill, knowledge, and potential of each individual and yourself for the manifestation process.

We all influence and are influenced by those around us, whether or not we intend it. The thoughts, feelings, attitudes, and beliefs of the people with whom you spend your time impress themselves upon you, especially when you lack confidence in your own beliefs and feelings. Therefore, it is important to choose wisely with whom you spend your time. Think about the people in your life—not just the people you consider important, but the people with whom you spend the most time. The following exercise can help you gain a clear perspective of how they may be influencing you.

Exercise 13: Knowing the People in Your Daily Life

Make a list of the six to eight people with whom you spend most of your time. These may not necessarily be the people you love the most or those you feel are most important to you. They are the people with whom you spend the most hours: fellow workers, colleagues, partners, family, friends. Think about each of these people, one at a time. What are they like? Be objective. Don't judge their integrity or character; just observe. As you consider each person, ask these questions:

- How does being around this person make you feel? Are you always happy to see them, or do you find yourself hoping to avoid them? Why?

- Does this person have a sense of who she is and what she wants in her life?

- Does this person entertain big ideas? Does he think "out of the box," or is he trapped in limiting belief systems?

- Is this person a high achiever, or satisfied with just enough to get by?

- If this person had a personal motto, what would it be? (Examples: "Anything is possible." "I hate change." "I'm always lucky." "Why is this happening to me?")

- Would you point this person out to others as a potential mentor or a powerful positive role model?

- Does spending time with this person leave you feeling uplifted and energized or are you relieved to get away from them?

- Does this person have something to gain in your staying just as you are, or do they encourage you to grow?

These may be lovely people with big hearts about whom you care deeply, but they may also be stuck or draining energy from you. If you are spending a lot of time with them, the challenge you face is to ward off their limiting thought patterns all the time. This burns up a lot of your energy that could be used for other pursuits.

After thinking about each of these people, choose several that you honestly feel can teach you something valuable—the ones you consider to be role models. In the coming days and weeks, focus your attention on how you can spend more time with and learn from these positive people.

Before you leave this exercise, bring to mind once again several of the people on your list. How would each of them answer those questions about you?

It is just as important to be surrounded by people who support you and your goals and call you forth to your greatest potential as it is for you to do that for them. This creates an environment of nurture, support, and empowerment. The more you live in that environment, the easier it is to remain focused on your project and to keep the energetic alignment necessary for manifestation. It is also helpful to have at least one person in your life who is farther along in their journey than you, someone with whom you can share ideas, someone you can admire and engage in stimulating conversation. A part of the work in the fifth house is making sure you have nurturing and mentoring people in your life, and that you are providing that energy for others as necessary for the manifestation of your vision.

The fifth house also calls you into leadership of your manifestation project. As the steward for your vision, you have already stepped into a leadership role in the project on some level. As you progress toward the sixth house, where you will design an action plan, you must fully claim the leadership role that your project requires. Everyone has a different comfort level in calling themselves a leader. What does leadership mean to you? Is it an easy role for you to assume or is stepping into leadership a challenge? Take time for the following exercise before we explore leadership further.

Exercise 14: Exploring Your Leadership Potential

You will need several sheets of blank paper and a pen for this exercise. Settle into a comfortable spot where you will not be disturbed for the next fifteen to thirty minutes, or perhaps more.

In the center of a blank sheet of paper, write the word "integrity" and draw a circle around it. Now write on this page every word that comes into your mind prompted by the word "integrity." When no more words arise, take the last word you wrote and start a new page with it. Write that word in the center of the page, draw a circle around it, and continue to free-associate, writing on this page every word that comes into your mind prompted by whatever word you wrote in the center. Continue this process until no more words come. Then take the last word you wrote and start a new page with it, following the same process. If at any point you have an "Aha!" moment, a revelation, a new understanding, or come up against a personal issue, stop free-associating. Take a fresh sheet of paper and write or draw that thought. If a specific revelation does not happen, continue the exercise until you have filled several pages. Stop and reflect on what you have written. What words surprise you? Why? How did it feel to do this exercise? What patterns do you notice in what you wrote? What do you learn about your relationship with integrity?

When you have completed your work with "integrity," go through the same process with the word "values," and then the word "leadership."

Finally, go through the same process with your full name, followed by the word "leader."

When you are finished, take time to settle into your Point of Stillness. When you reach the silence, consider the following questions. Take time to sit with each question and, when you are ready, go to your journal to write.

- Do you consider yourself a person of integrity? How does your integrity show up in your interactions with others? Are there places where you lack integrity? What changes do you need to make in those places in order to regain it?

- What are your core values?

- As this manifestation project unfolds, does it remain in alignment with your core values or are your values being compromised in any way? If they are being compromised, what needs to shift to bring your project or vision back into alignment with your values?

- Do you consider yourself a leader? Are you comfortable with the idea of being a leader?

- What have you learned about yourself in this exercise? What have you learned about your relationhip with leadership?

Becoming a Leader

There are three fundamental phases to becoming a leader: following a leader, self-leadership, and leading others. Before you can become a leader, you must follow other leaders to learn, grow, and develop. At some point, you advance to the second phase, personal leadership, in which you become the leader of your own life. You may or may not ever choose to step formally into the third phase of leadership, leading others. If you want to manifest visions, accomplish goals, and see projects through to the end, however, you must ultimately become at least the leader of your own life. No one else can do that for you. In the final analysis, you must decide what you will make of your life and how you will claim responsibility for seeing your projects through to manifestation.

There are some common characteristics that most successful leaders embody. First and foremost, a leader has a clear vision. Without that clarity, there is nowhere to go, no sense of direction. You declared an intention in the first house and set out in a particular direction toward your project. In each successive house, that vision has progressed in some way toward manifestation. In the fourth house, you chose a specific path on which to focus from among several possibilities. Now, in the fifth house, you are called to an even deeper commitment to that intention and to your project. Here, you step more fully into leading the way toward its manifestation. Furthermore, as the leader for your manifestation project, you must be sincere, passionate, and articulate as you share your vision with others. You must clearly communicate the importance of the vision being manifested. The energy is building now, and you may be called upon to speak about your vision in more public ways as you align the energy and conditions for it to manifest.

A leader also builds bridges between people and ideas. It may be essential to your project that certain people or organizations support it. Yet some of those people may not understand it fully. The fifth house calls you to articulate your vision clearly to create the alliances you need, and to encourage those who are hesitant to get on board.

This house also calls you to be a mediator when conflicts or challenges arise—the level-headed one who can hear every side of a story and help those involved hear one another. This includes finding harmony between conflicting beliefs and desires within yourself. In some ways, the fifth house takes the energy of the second house to a higher level. The stakes are getting higher now. You are well into the manifestation process. This often means being the compassionate observer, being rooted in your high-heart center (see chapter 4), as well as compassionately observing yourself. This is an invaluable skill when you are challenged to identify and articulate uncomfortable truths—to call reality what it is and work with the truth of a situation. As a compassionate observer, you can help others and yourself face and work through whatever the uncomfortable truth may be in order to best serve the manifestation of your vision's potential. Once you begin creating and implementing your action plan in the sixth house, it will be harder to turn back. The fifth house is where you make sure that everything for your project is truly in alignment on every level before you dive into action.

A true leader empowers everyone around them to be the best they can be. Empowering others means illuminating their strengths and potentials, and helping them see how they can develop those qualities. As you empower others, you empower yourself, because you create an energetic space in which everyone is operating at their best. You create an environment where everyone aims high and sets the highest standard. You do this, not by creating stress and pressure to produce, but by creating excitement and desire among everyone involved to develop themselves to their absolute best and offer their best to the world, in thought and in action.

Finally, as the leader of your manifestation project, you must ensure that the momentum continues to build. You must inspire and motivate others. As momentum builds, everyone involved gets excited; as the excitement grows, it creates even more momentum.

To be a leader, you must have a personal commitment to movement and action toward your vision. Too many people want the benefit of the manifestation without doing the work or taking the action. A true leader realizes that nothing is accomplished without doing the work. As we have stressed over and over, in the manifestation paradigm, a huge percentage of that work is done in your thoughts. Consider that you are more than half-way around the Manifestation Wheel and still have not come to the House of Action. Most of your work thus far has been in the unseen world of thought, feeling, energy, and concept. Only after you have worked through the "inner stuff" to align thought, intention, belief, and decision with potential are you truly ready for action in the three-dimensional world.

We were all born to do different things, to fulfill different soul missions, and to manifest different visions. However, no matter what talents you are given at birth, those talents must be developed and refined. The same is true with leadership. When you look at your project and recognize who you must be, how you must focus your energy and thought, and what conditions must be created in order to manifest your vision, you discover what talents and skills you must develop to provide the necessary leadership for your particular project. Look for others who can serve as role models for who you want to be. You don't have to know them personally. Who do you want to emulate in your life? Choose your mentors carefully, and then learn everything you can from them—from their mistakes as well as their successes.

Your manifestation project communicates a message to the world. The fifth house asks you to be clear about what that message is, and ensure that it is indeed the message you want to convey. Here, you must also make sure that the message is in harmony with the greatest potential of your project.

Take time to journal about the following questions:

- What is the message that people are getting as I manifest this vision?

- Is this the message I want them to receive?

- How does the manifestation of this vision serve me directly? What are its gifts?

- How does the manifestation of this vision serve others? What are its gifts for them? What message does it carry to the community about who I am?

Another important consideration around nurture, leadership, and empowerment in manifestation is how and where you create and honor personal boundaries, especially concerning your project. In all of the activities of the fifth house, there is a fine line between not doing enough and going overboard by doing too much—between offering yourself to your project and others and losing yourself in the process.

Setting clear boundaries is one of the greatest gifts you can give to yourself, to those you are working with, and to your project. By honoring your personal space, needs, desires, and vision, you encourage others to honor theirs. You cannot manifest another's vision for them, or protect them from the life lessons they are here to learn. You cannot take on their feelings for them or protect them from hurt. Nor can they do that for you. However, you can ensure that you are always acting with integrity and compassion, holding everyone in their greatest light. Understanding and embracing this concept allows you to set boundaries that can ultimately empower everyone involved. It is then up to each individual whether they accept the empowerment or not.

Part of the work of the fifth house is to recognize the role you have taken on for your project and the way others perceive you. It is important to consider:

- Is this a role you want to play?

- Is this how you want to be seen by others?

- Does playing this role enrich your life, or is it costing you in some way?

- Is the role you have taken on truly serving your vision?

- Does your playing of that role help others to be all that they can be?

Without clear self-awareness and willingness to ask the hard questions and speak the uncomfortable truths, nurture, leadership, and service can devolve into co-dependence. You can find yourself taking on roles or living out patterns that keep you and others around you comfortable and protected from challenges you don't want to face. Or you can find yourself in a role you took on long ago, not realizing or thinking about the long-term consequences. These hard questions must be addressed here in the fifth house so that you can enter the House of Action unencumbered by roles and titles that are in conflict with your project or vision.

As you consider how nurture, leadership, and empowerment fit into your particular manifestation project, examine your true motives. Why are you taking any particular action of nurture, leadership, or empowerment? Be clear that you are making choices based on stewarding the greatest potential of your vision and calling forth the greatest potential from everyone involved.

Be honest with yourself about what you can and cannot do. When you overspend your time, energy, money, or self, eventually everyone involved in the project suffers. Don't compare yourself with what others are able to do or choose to do. That is their journey. You have your own journey. Be true to it, to your available energy, to your heart, and to the greatest potential available to you.

Keep your communication open and honest with everyone involved in the project. Breakdown or lack of communication is the cause of most problems. When something needs to be said, speak it clearly, simply, and honestly from your heart. Ask that you be heard from the heart. And offer the same gift to everyone else.

Know your priorities and honor them. When you are called to play a role or take on a task that feels in conflict with your project or that will take you away from the potential, say "no." Let go of things that are not really yours to do, at least for now. When people ask for something that you cannot give, refer them to someone who can. Honor your vision and your commitment to stewarding its potential.

The House of Empowerment is the last step before you design, create, and implement an action plan. In this house, you "step up to the plate" and re-commit to your project at new levels. As you prepare to move into the House of Action, you are about to bring your vision into physical manifestation. It's about to become real. At the point that potential becomes form, it takes on a three-dimensional life of its own. The House of Empowerment is your last check to be sure that, on an energetic level, everything is in place and that you feel good about where you are going and what you are manifesting. Before moving into the House of Action, take time to journal about the following questions:

- How does this project call you to be all that you can be? How does it challenge you to grow in positive and constructive ways?

- How does your project call everyone involved to be all they can be? How does it challenge them to grow in positive and constructive ways?

- Is there any way in which your project manipulates anyone, including yourself, to be someone they are not?

- Is there anything about this project or its process that could cause harm to anyone or to any group or organization?

- What leadership skills or characteristics do you need to develop or refine to accomplish your goal?

- Do you like who you are becoming as you pursue this project?

- As you look at others involved in the project, do you like who they are becoming through this process?

- House #1 Check-in: How does your work in this house help you see and commit to your vision more clearly?

- House #2 Check-in: After your work in this house, has your sense of peace around the manifestation of your vision been compromised in any way? If so, what needs to shift?

- House #3 Check-in: After your work in this house, do you feel more or less enthusiasm and motivation for the accomplishment of your vision? If less, what needs to shift?

- House #4 Check-in: After your work in this house, do you see your future any differently? If so, how is it guiding you? Does anything need to shift?

CHAPTER 8

House #6: Action

Create an initial action plan.
Implement the plan.

At last we come to the sixth house: Action. Time to create a plan and put it into motion. There are several characteristics of a manifestation action plan that distinguish it from a traditional plan. First, your intuitive understanding of the potential of the project itself, the guidance you receive from aligning with that potential and Consciousness, and your experience of remembering the future and letting it show you the way. These characteristics greatly inform the design and creation of your plan and expand it far beyond the intellectual approach of "figuring it out." Second, in a manifestation action plan, you focus on who you are within the implementation of the plan, and on maintaining alignment of your thoughts, beliefs, intentions, decisions, and actions with the energetic potential. Finally, the implementation of the plan continues to be guided by the potential until full manifestation has been accomplished.

It's important to note that what you create in the sixth house is your initial action plan—your first draft—a place to begin. The plan will become a living, breathing entity. Its breath and life force are the potential of your project. As you work the plan, the project evolves, the potential unfolds, and you see the path toward manifestation more and more clearly. Therefore, the plan you create now may very well be adjusted, amended, altered, and reconsidered a few, if not many, times.

Many of the pieces of your action plan may already be in place; others you may have no idea of at the moment. Not all steps along the path may be clear as you begin. This is completely normal. You'll discover them as you go along. There is an element of mystery and magic to the manifestation process. It is important to keep this in mind, so that you don't put off getting started because you can't yet see every step. Even if you think you know all of the steps to the full manifestation of your vision, there is still a very good chance that something will happen along the way that you don't expect. And that's where you learn and grow. Both life and your project will present you with surprising turns. Some may even be significant challenges. But if you take those challenges into the silence and work with them as you did when you created reality fields in the third house and opportunities in the second and fourth houses, they can catapult you toward your goal.

The more passion and commitment you have for your project, the more closely aligned it is with your soul and, therefore, the more likely it is to contain significant lessons and opportunities for growth and transformation. You don't need to worry now about what they may be; they'll appear if and when their time is right. Your job is to remain focused and committed, and to recognize and embrace the lessons and opportunities when they arise.

So let's begin creating your action plan. You will need a notebook or a laptop computer to capture components of the plan as you discover them.

Pause at each step of the process to make notes. If you are using paper for your notes, use a separate page for each step of the process so that you can come back and add more notes later. Give yourself plenty of time for this process—at least a couple of hours—and you will find it exciting, inspiring, and empowering. Let the momentum build as you go along and, if you start to get overwhelmed with all there is to do, pause and take a few deep breaths before you continue. Push through. Take a short break if you need it, but not so long that you lose your focus.

Begin to map your action plan by going to the future, a year after your project has been completed and your vision fully manifested. Then work backward from that time, discovering what was accomplished and/or what transpired at various time markers. Through this process, you co-create a map or framework for your action plan with the future, Consciousness, and the potential of your project. Then go back and fill in details as they become clearer. Most important, have fun with this process. Let it be playful, creative, intuitive, and exciting. You may want to read through the next exercise before you begin working, then return to the beginning and proceed one paragraph at a time.

Exercise 15: Discovering Your Action Plan Map

Find a spacious area, indoors or out, in which you can move around for this exercise. Have your paper and pen or laptop computer nearby, then take a few moments to settle into your Point of Stillness.

Choose a spot to represent the present time. Stand in that spot and state your intention from the first house or your revised intention if it has evolved since you began your manifestation journey. Acknowledge the current status of your project or vision and pay particular attention to how the project feels to you right now. What is the current reality field?

Now, as if "fast-forwarding" through time, walk to a spot that you choose to represent a year after your project is complete, your vision manifested. Make sure there is a good distance between the starting and end points for your project so that you have plenty of room to discover points of time in between.

Settle into the spot representing one year after your project is complete, take a few deep and full breaths, and feel the energy of this time and space. Take in as much as you can about how it feels to be in the space where you've been living with your fully manifested vision for a year, then consider the following questions:

- What is the outcome of your manifestation project?

- How is the outcome a vehicle or vessel for the greatest potential of the project?

- How did the manifestation happen? Was the process arduous or relatively smooth? Did you work on your own or with others? As you look back on the process from the perspective of a year later, what is important about how it happened?

- What has been the impact of your manifestation project on your life and circumstances?

- What has been the impact of your project on others?

- What does this tell you about your project?

Take time to record your impressions before continuing.

When you are ready, walk back in the direction of your starting place and choose a spot that represents the time when your manifestation project has just been completed. What is your first impression of the date? Don't be surprised if the date you receive is sooner or later than you had in mind. Just accept what comes for now, take a few deep and full breaths, and celebrate the completion of your manifestation project. Feel the energy and describe it. What is the reality field now that the project has just been completed? Reflect on the manifestation journey you have just completed:

- How was it? Having just completed the manifestation process, what are you celebrating the most?

- With the manifestation process so fresh in your mind, what do you now know about it?

- What were the critical components of the manifestation process, both in thought and in action?

Take plenty of time to make sure you are grounded in the reality field of full manifestation, then record your impressions.

Before continuing, do a little time calculation. Divide the total length of time that your project took to complete into shorter action periods. For example, if the length of time from start to finish was one year, divide that into six two-month action periods. If your project took six months to complete, divide that into six one-month periods. If your manifestation project took longer than a year, divide the time into two-month action periods for the first year and six-month periods beyond the first year. If your current project only took a couple of months or less, your action periods may be days or weeks instead of months.

There is no right or wrong way to do this. Use your intuition and take a few moments to determine what the best action periods are for your project.

Now work backward from the completion date to specific time markers, each marking the end of an action period. At each marker, visit that time and take note of what has been accomplished to date, gathering as many details as you can. For example, if your project completion date is September 1 and you are using two-month action periods, July 1 is your first time marker, May 1 the second, and so on. Begin by walking backward to the spot that represents July 1 and explore that time and space, what was accomplished by this time, and how it was accomplished. Gather as much information as possible about where your project or vision is at this date.

At each time marker, remember that you are co-creating this plan by letting the project and its potential show you what has been accomplished rather than projecting or predicting what happens. Stay in your intuitive mind for this entire process and you will be shown the way. Your role at this point of the co-creative process is to gather all the intuitive information and organize it into a written plan or map.

Now choose a spot to represent your first time marker—the one closest to the final completion of the project—and walk to that spot. Standing in the spot, take a few moments to settle into this space and time. Take deep and full breaths and feel the energy here. Then consider these questions:

- What has been accomplished for your project by this time?

- How did you do it? What specific thoughts, actions, and choices led you to this point?

- Who was involved in the project to date, and what were their roles?

- Where did the resources come from—time, money, and assistance?

- What else do you need to ask from this space relevant to your particular project and its action plan?

Take time to record all the information you have gathered before moving on to the next time marker.

When you are ready, make your way backward in time by walking to the spot that represents the next time marker. Take a few moments to settle into this space and time. Take deep and full breaths and feel the energy here, then consider the questions above for this point in your manifestation process. Once again, record all the information you have gathered before you move on to the next time marker.

Continue this process at every time marker, until you are at the time marker closest to your starting point. After gathering all the information you can there, divide your last time span into increasingly shorter action periods. For example, if you have been working in two-month action periods, set time markers now for six weeks into the project, then a month, and then weekly markers for the first month of your action plan. This will give you a more detailed starting plan. Then walk backward in time, visiting each time marker and gathering information, until you make your way back to the starting point.

Once you arrive at the starting point, take a few moments to celebrate what you have just done! You've just co-created a map for your action plan. And you did it by letting the project and its potential show you the way. That is a huge accomplishment. As you implement the plan, you will add more details and flesh it out, but you now have a great overall map and direction.

Go back now to the notes you took from your masterminding session in the third house and your visit to the future in the fourth house. You may want to add some of your discoveries from those processes to your action plan. Ask the plan which of these components belong in this map you have just created, and where.

Then go back through your action map and list the resources you will need at each step along the way. Create an intention for them to show up when they are needed.

Finally, review the action map once more so that it starts to become a part of you. If there are aspects of the plan that still feel incomplete, that's alright. Chances are they are farther down the road. It may not yet be time to fill in the details for them. Other things may need to happen first, at which point, the details will become clear. Take the plan as it is now and dive in. You're on your way!

Implementing Your Plan

As you begin putting your action plan into motion, it is important to stay in dialog with the potential and work with the energy. Remember that you started out your manifestation journey by asking: What wants to happen? If you have been true to the co-creative process all the way through, there is an inherent forward motion already present in your project because it is what wants to happen. Therefore, if you continue to keep everything in alignment, to hold the reality field and create the conditions in which the potential will manifest and thrive, the biggest part of the work is done. The potential will unfold into form because that's what it wants to do. The more you can remain in dialog with the potential and the project and resist the temptation to analyze, intellectualize, or force an outcome, the easier and faster things will happen.

Flexibility is important as you implement your plan. Unexpected things will happen, some things will take longer than expected, and others will happen very quickly. You and the potential are co-creating a new form, as if you are in a dance together. As the steward and leader for your project, sometimes you lead the dance; at other times, the potential takes the lead. Things are moving now and you have to ride the wave. Sometimes you may need to step back and let things happen; at other times, you must charge ahead. The key is to remain focused and let the task and the project show you what needs to be done next. As you reach each time marker in the implementation process, pause to revise the plan as needed before entering the next action period. Use the process you have just completed as a model for filling in the details of each new action period. Break that period down into shorter intervals and then walk backward through those time intervals. This process will show you the map for the next action period.

As you implement your action plan, it is important to make the best use of your time and energy. This demands a clear awareness of how you spend your time each day and what activities and responsibilities are claiming top priority. Make choices consciously and be proactive in time management. Keep your project a top priority in time and focus. Don't let yourself get lost in others' agendas or situations. Honor your commitment to your project and its potential.

Time management is not just about scheduling and prioritizing things to do, however. The master time manager also recognizes the importance of creating empty time in the day—time to just "be," time for entering the silence and listening to your intuition, allowing your soul and your project to speak to you and guide you. Empty time also gives room for ideas, people, and circumstances to present themselves at the perfect time for the continued unfolding of your vision.

Finally, you must also create time in your life for whatever it is that you want to manifest. For instance, if you want to manifest more time for your family, but insist on scheduling appointments seven days a week from 8:00 A.M. to 10:00 P.M., there is little space left for family time to materialize. If you want to manifest a new job, but you don't tell anyone you are interested in another position or allow time for a job search and interviews, there is much less chance that the job will appear.

Once you have created the space for your project or vision, let your imagination take you into that space. Specialized photography has shown that, before the root of a plant extends, it projects its energy out into the space it will inhabit. The heart of a fetus begins as a cell that has a pulse or beat long before the heart has formed. The idea of a heart was present first and the cell was infused with that idea. You have now created an action plan to bring your vision into physical reality. Make sure that there is space into which it can materialize. Fill that space with your energy and intention, then take the action necessary to complete the manifestation.

Through your action plan, you are empowered to manifest your vision. From this point, all you have to do is *do it*. You must follow through. You must discipline yourself and stay vigilant in your plan. You've done the inner work; you've cleared away energetic blocks and belief patterning; you've learned to become the master of your thought. Now the time has come to put it into practice, to walk the walk of your vision or project. By stepping into action, you put yourself on the line. Your commitment is no longer limited to thought, intention, and choices. By setting your plan in motion, you commit to action.

As you implement your plan, you may come up against risks and challenges you didn't foresee. Your greatest fears or resistance often come just as you reach a point of tremendous breakthrough or powerful initiation. On some level of consciousness, you realize that your life may not be the same once you pass through that gate. So you resist, reluctant to give up something of the past or something you know, or to do something that could change the course of your life. However, the point at which that resistance arises is precisely the time to take a deep breath and walk on. The Chinese character for crisis means both opportunity and danger. So it is in your journey. What you most desire is often also what you most fear. Manifesting great dreams often demands summoning great courage to step into your most profound potential and begin living it.

That said, when you know, deep in your heart, that something isn't right, honor that knowing. At any point in the action planning and implementation process, you can still go back to your intention and make revisions if something doesn't feel right. Honor your commitment to your project and its potential and if, after clear consideration, it seems time to change course, follow the guidance of the project and your soul and take the action that feels right to you.

One last, but important, aspect of the sixth house is gratitude. As you begin to implement your action plan, be grateful for each day's accomplishments—in fact, for all the gifts life brings you. Gratitude increases the flow of energy in your life. A regular practice of gratitude can open the floodgates of abundance a little wider each day. Give thanks for the opportunity to share your gifts and to experience all that life offers. Express your gratitude for everything in your life: your home, your family and friends, the money that flows through your life, the challenges you face and the gifts within those challenges, the experiences of your day. As a part of your time management, create a few minutes each day to sit quietly, breathe, and give thanks. You will see the abundance of your life greatly increase.

To wrap up your work in the sixth house, take time to check in with the previous houses:

- House #1 Check-in: Having created an action plan, has anything shifted in your understanding of your vision or project? Does anything in your intention and/or commitment need to change? If so, what?

- House #2 Check-in: Does your action plan in any way compromise your sense of inner peace? If so, what needs to shift?

- House #3 Check-in: Does your action plan create more or less enthusiasm and motivation for your project? If less, what needs to shift?

- House #4 Check-in: Is your action plan in harmony with what you have seen of the future? If not, what needs to shift?

- House #5 Check-in: How does the implementation of your action plan nurture, empower, and add value to your life and to the lives of others?

Once you have completed your action plan map and the steps of your first action period are clear, you may want to put that first period on its own Manifestation Wheel. If there seem to be several components to that first action period, you can even start a new Wheel for each one. You have done a huge amount of work on your overall project, so most, if not all, of your action plan components will go around the Wheel very quickly. You've worked out all of the big issues. Just give it the time it needs, and you will accomplish the goal easily and efficiently.

Again, congratulations! You have just completed what very few people ever take the time to do. You have created a plan. And even fewer people intentionally co-create that plan with potential and the greater Consciousness. Put your plan into action now, and watch your vision become reality.

CHAPTER 9

House #7: Surrender

Surrender to the manifestation process.
Live intuitively.
Trust that the project will be taken where it needs to go.
Expect synergy and synchronicity as a natural way of living.
Follow the energy.

There comes a time in the manifestation process when you have done all you can do. You aligned thought, intention, belief, choice, and action with potential. You created a potent reality field. You created an action plan and set it into motion. Your project is taking on a life of its own now and, unless you suddenly feel it is headed in the wrong direction, it's time to surrender to the momentum and let it and the project lead the way. Your job in the seventh house is to follow the energy and serve your vision as it takes form.

Within the context of the manifestation process, surrender has a different meaning than the one we usually give it. It doesn't mean giving up or giving in. It means giving over—giving yourself over completely to what wants to happen—and committing yourself to the service of your project and following its lead. All of your preparation and work has led you to this point.

Now you must ride the energy. It's a powerful and exciting time. It can be unsettling at times if you aren't sure where the momentum is taking you or exactly how it's all going to turn out. But if you ride the wave of momentum and potential and continue in service to the greatest possible outcome of that potential, chances are good that you will manifest something equal to or better than you originally hoped.

We have emphasized many times that energy alignment is the key to manifestation. Your success at becoming a master of manifestation and co-creation lies in your ability to do three things: align thought, intention, belief, decision, and action with potential; surrender to the wave of momentum that rises out of that alignment and then ride that wave; and create an energetic space where synergy and synchronicity are considered normal and miracles are a part of everyday life, and then surrender to that synergistic process. When you are successful, you create an energetic space and then surrender to what happens in that space.

The seventh house marks the beginning of the most magical and amazing part of your manifestation journey. Until now, you have been receiving guidance from potential and actively putting things in place so that the potential has everything it needs to manifest. In essence, until now, you've been setting up the right conditions for manifestation. In the seventh house, you step back and let the potential unfold through the favorable conditions you have created. Make no mistake; you will still be fully engaged in the service of your vision. Now, however, you let synergy and synchronicity do their magic. You turn your vision over to unseen forces and to the potential itself once again, and a new level of co-creation begins. You recognize that you are not alone in this manifestation process. The entire web of Consciousness supports you. Indeed, the web that connects everything to everything else makes that synergy and synchronicity possible.

Surrender means letting go of control and allowing your project to have a life of its own. As your project manifests, it will continue to ask things of you. In the sixth house, you sometimes called the shots in the implementation of your action plan; at others, the potential led the way. Sometimes you were actively engaged in moving things forward; at others, you stepped out of the way to let things unfold as they would. This co-creative partnership is not unlike a relay race, in which a team of runners all work together to reach the finish line. One runner begins the race carrying the baton. At a certain point on the path, the first runner hands the baton off to a second runner and stops to rest. The second then carries it the next distance, then passes it off to someone else, or perhaps back to the first runner. The team is always fully participating in the race, even though, at any particular time, only one person is actually running.

From the very beginning of your manifestation journey in the first house, you have passed your project idea—your "baton"—back and forth with Consciousness, aligning energy and creating the conditions to support its successful manifestation, almost as if you were getting everything ready for the race to begin, setting everything in place, and doing all you could to remove and avoid obstacles. In the sixth house, the race began. You designed your action plan and set it into motion. As you worked your plan, you passed the baton back and forth, sometimes between yourself and unseen co-creation forces—Consciousness and potential—and sometimes between yourself and other physical co-creation partners like colleagues or subcontractors.

In the seventh house, you may recognize that multiple partners are holding onto ends of the baton at the same time.

Multiple action steps are being taken in the physical realm and, at the same time, things are happening synergistically and synchronistically in the unseen realm. Your job now is to surrender control of the project to the energy and momentum that is carrying it. Just as in a relay race the energy and momentum of the race itself support and sustain the runners, the momentum and synergy of the manifestation process will support and sustain you if you surrender to them and allow them to work their magic.

You have probably experienced this when working on a project with a group. Early in the process, the group functions as a single entity in partnership with an idea. As action progresses, the members of the group take on individual roles, partnering and co-creating, not only with each other, but with the idea in order to complete the project. Each person plays a very significant role in the completion of the project, yet no one person alone makes the project happen. In the best teamwork, each person surrenders to the momentum of the project and recognizes they are just one part of a much larger energy that fuels everyone involved. Surrender, in the seventh house, means surrendering to the manifestation process, recognizing that you are just one partner of many engaged in co-creation. Even if you are the only person directly working on your manifestation project, the project itself, its potential, and Consciousness are still your co-creative partners. The more you develop your intuitive awareness, the more you will sense when the time is right for a particular action—to make the phone call, to send the press release, to remove the safety net and let the project fly on its own.

The surrender of the seventh house also allows you to rest. You no longer have to carry the baton all the time. You don't have to run every stretch of the race. You do your part, and then you pass the baton off to someone else, to the potential or to Consciousness, or perhaps even to all three—and you trust that things will continue to unfold. Then you rest and prepare for the time when the baton will be passed back to you.

In Command or In Control?

While in a manifestation process you are never really "in control" of the project, the seventh house asks you to relinquish any lingering hold you may have on it and learn what it means to be "in command" rather than in control. When you are in control, you keep a firm grip on every aspect of your project so that nothing can happen without your direct involvement. You are "making it happen." When you are in command, on the other hand, you surrender control and "dance" with all of the many components and partners. You may still be the principal steward for this vision, but you have many co-creative partners, in both the physical and nonphysical dimensions. Many things may happen without you being involved at all.

Surrendering control of your project opens the door to co-creative partnership as perhaps you have never known it. Early in the journey, you learned that the potential needs you as its partner and steward in order to cross the bridge from energy into form. At the same time, you need the potential as your inspiration and guide. From the beginning, there has been an interdependent relationship between you and the potential. However, the roles within that relationship shift as you get closer to manifesting your project or goal. The more the potential takes form in the three-dimensional world, the less it needs you to cross the bridge from the unseen world. It now knows the way across. While you let the potential guide you in thought and preparation, you were still making the decisions for action and intention in the three-dimensional world. But now, synchronicities occur, things fall into place, and it seems as if the project itself is making choices and decisions to which you must respond. Following the energy means surrendering to the project and the life it takes on, being less a steward and more a support. Your co-creative partnership roles have evolved.

All of this, however, is only the beginning of the surrender called for in the seventh house. Here you also consider your project within the larger context of your life and where you are now—the lessons you are learning, the skills you are developing or refining, the gifts you are giving. This house asks you to look at your project within the context of your soul mission or life purpose. It asks you to consider to what you must surrender in the bigger picture of your life to more fully realize your personal potential in the world. The seventh house broadens your perspective on your vision and its manifestation process so that you understand its place within the greater unfolding of your life.

Take some time to journal about the following questions:

- How does your vision or project fit into the larger context of your life? How does it relate to your ongoing journey?

- How does your vision or project relate to your soul mission or life purpose?

- To what must you surrender in order to more fully realize your greatest potential?

From the context of your life and soul mission, the seventh house calls you to awareness of the bigger "what wants to happen" for the greater good of all. It calls you to be aware of your project and its potential within the bigger picture of the universal potential, and then to surrender to that universal "what wants to happen" as well as to the energy of your vision.

Through this larger surrender, energy alignment occurs on a grand scale. Now the greater Consciousness does the heavy work, supporting the potential and you. There is no more powerful co-creative partner. When co-creating with the greater Consciousness becomes a natural part of your life, you have indeed mastered the art of co-creation.

Again, take time to journal about the following questions:

- When you tap into "what wants to happen" for the greater good, how does your project fit into that context?

- What would it mean for your project and for your life to surrender to the universal potential—the greatest potential available at this time for the good of all?

Living Intuitively

In the fourth house, you tapped into your intuition to visit the future, asking to be shown possible outcomes for your vision. You transcended linear time and moved into the realm of Consciousness, where past, present, and future all co-exist, and where things exist only as ideas, not in specific forms or locations. Now you move to a new relationship with intuition. The seventh house invites you to *live* intuitively—to engage in an ongoing conversation with your soul, with Consciousness, and with the greatest potential in any situation or circumstance—not just to tap into your intuition from time to time. It invites you into an ongoing awareness that, on one level of reality, everything that has ever happened or will ever happen is happening now. When you live in that ongoing awareness, remembering the future and calling its energetic essence into the present becomes a normal part of life. In any moment, you can step into the simultaneous time/space realm of Consciousness, choose what you need—knowledge or understanding, belief or circumstance—and bring it back across the bridge to this linear and physical time/space reality.

Although you may not realize it, you constantly step back and forth between linear and simultaneous time/space awareness. Any time you fantasize or daydream, you shift out of the linear realm. You consciously began practicing that shift with the Point of Stillness meditation in the first house of the Manifestation Wheel. As you progressed around the Wheel, your work in many of the houses included shifting out of a linear time/space dimension. Though shifting time and space may seem impossible to the rational mind, once you are willing to surrender your rational thought to your larger intuitive mind, it happens naturally.

Your intuitive mind encompasses your rational mind, yet is far from being limited by it. When well developed, it is able to function simultaneously in a linear time/space dimension and a boundary-free, simultaneous time/space dimension. The capacity to move back and forth between the linear and non-linear worlds is a part of our design as humans. Just because, as a culture, we have lost touch with that capacity does not mean that individuals can't develop it. As more individuals reclaim that capacity, it can become a part of our culture once again, just as it was in many ancient cultures and still is in some non-Western cultures. Meditation is the gateway to this boundary-free dimension. As you develop your meditation skills, you can become a master at time/space travel, breaking the bonds of time and space to gain new perspectives and access other realities.

The more adept you become at interacting with the world through your intuitive mind, the more easily you shift back and forth between the linear time/space dimension and the boundary-free realm. Your judgment about what is or is not possible in the energetic realm disappears. You recognize that, in fact, all possibilities exist there and it is up to you to choose those with which you want to partner. Living intuitively requires the surrender of your rational mind to the larger intuitive mind. It means stepping beyond a process that is limited to "thinking," into one that involves all of your inner and outer senses— "intuiting" life. It means living in a reality where multiple futures exist simultaneously and where you regularly access the guidance and wisdom you need from the greater Consciousness.

The following meditation exercise adapts the highway metaphor from chapter 6 and offers a tool to help you more easily move between linear and simultaneous space/time. Surrender to the possibility that you can do this, and see what new awareness this exercise brings you.

Exercise 16: Traveling through Time/Space

Go once again to your Point of Stillness. Once you are settled there, imagine a very long, straight highway with nothing alongside it. The highway stretches beyond the limits of your sight in both directions.

Allow your imagination to turn that highway into a timeline. Traveling back and forth along this highway represents the passage of time, from the distant past to the distant future. Imagine that everything that has ever happened or ever will happen lies somewhere on this linear time highway.

Imagine the point on the highway that represents this present moment in time, and place yourself in that spot. As you stand there and look in the direction of the future, imagine that, just ahead of this moment in time, the highway divides into many lanes that head off in different directions—different possibilities of how the future could unfold. From your present position, you can see only a short distance into the future—however far your rational mind can imagine. If you turn around to look toward the past, you can perhaps see a bit farther back in time—just what your conscious memory allows. You are experiencing as much access to the linear timeline as your rational mind allows.

Now float up in your awareness until you are several hundred feet above the highway. From this perspective, you can see much more of the highway or timeline. You can see much farther into both the past and the future, including many possibilities of how things may unfold, because you can see where some of the lanes of the future end up. As you float higher, you can see increasingly greater expanses of the linear time highway. From this high vantage point, however, something else magical happens. You not only can perceive the past and the future; as you perceive it, it is all happening at once! The higher you rise above the highway, the less it is a timeline and the more it is simply a very long road with millions of people, places, and events happening all at once in the same space. Take your time to really experience this.

When you are ready, ask to be shown where the complete manifestation of your project or vision lies within this big picture of past, present, and future. Where on the highway does it appear? From this higher perspective, how do you see your project or vision fitting into the bigger scheme of things?

There is nothing difficult about expanding to this awareness. All it demands is a willingness to let go of what you were always taught was real. It simply demands that you suspend rational thought and surrender to the possibility of a greater reality.

Remain in this expanded awareness for a while, either in silence, or writing in your journal. The more you practice this meditation exercise, the more adept you will become at rising quickly above the linear time highway and shifting to a simultaneous time/space view. Then you can easily jump back and forth between these two perspectives. With this skill, you gain the ability to perceive life as a simultaneous process; you are no longer trapped within the confines of the linear time/space dimension. You can visit the simultaneous time/space realm, gather what you need, and bring it back with you into the linear time/space world.

Living in this expanded awareness gives you a much greater perspective and understanding of process. You can see the future, experience it energetically, and gain a perspective of when things will happen and how. You can perceive multiple outcomes simultaneously and choose to travel in the lane that will take you to a chosen outcome. And because you have seen the future, you can trust that things will unfold in their own time.

Everything in life operates in cycles and flows of energy. The seventh house asks you to surrender to those flows and cycles. There are energetic forces at work that you will never fully understand in your human experience. However, as these unseen forces kick in, things happen. The seventh house asks you to surrender to those forces—to let go and to trust them, and then to step back into action when responsibility is handed back to you.

The seventh house asks you to surrender to the many levels of guidance that are available to you, and to live in the faith that you will know where to be and when to be there when something is ready to happen. The right circumstances will appear, you will recognize them, and you will know the role you are to play. This house invites you to live intuitively, which demands discipline and practice—time in meditation, reflection, and introspection; time in communion with your soul, the greater Consciousness, and the greatest potential of your project.

To wrap up your work in the seventh house, take time to journal about the following questions:

- Are you making time and space for regular meditation, introspection, and reflection? Are you engaging in intuitive conversation with your soul, Consciousness, and the potential of your project? If so, what is that like? If not, how can you get started?

- Have you made the transition from tapping into intuition from time to time to *living* intuitively? If so, how do you experience that? If not, how can you begin?

- Are you surrendering your vision to the unseen forces to allow synergy and synchronicity to occur? If so, what are you experiencing? If not, what do you need to be able to fully surrender? How can that happen?

- House #1 Check-in: Has anything shifted in your intention and personal commitments as a result of surrendering to your project and its momentum as well as the universal potential of this time?

- House #2 Check-in: Has your work in the seventh house in any way compromised your sense of inner peace? If so, what needs to shift?

- House #3 Check-in: Do you have more or less enthusiasm and motivation for your project after your work in the seventh house? If less, what needs to shift?

- House #4 Check-in: How has your work in this house impacted your vision of the future? Does anything need to shift?

- House #5 Check-in: Through your work in this house, do you continue to see how your project will nurture and add value to your life and the lives of others?

- House #6 Check-in: As you surrender on deeper and higher levels, does your action plan need any adjustment? If so, what adjustments need to be made?

The seventh house helps you see that your vision or project is a vehicle for creation on multiple levels. When you enter the higher levels of co-creation, you surrender your personal vision to the greater potential of our evolving culture and civilization. This doesn't mean you have to settle for less. On the contrary. It means that you are expanding into the universal Consciousness and actively participating in the ongoing co-creation and evolution of your world. You see your vision or project within a much larger context, and become an active participant in the synergistic dance of co-creation with Consciousness.

CHAPTER 10

House #8: Legacy

Consider the impact of your project on the future.
Consider the legacy created by your project and your life.
Consider the sustainability of your project
for now and for the future.

The elders of the Iroquois Confederacy taught that, in our every deliberation, we must consider the impact of our decisions on the next seven generations. Decisions must be made and actions taken based, not only on immediate needs and desires, but on the impact they may have on the lives of our grandchildren's grandchildren. In the traditional Balinese culture, they believe that we reincarnate every seventh generation. Therefore, they make choices and decisions based on the belief that they will be back again and will have to live with the consequences of their actions.

The eighth and final house of the Manifestation Wheel calls you to consider your project or vision from this long-term perspective. It takes the considerations of the House of Empowerment—how your project nurtures and empowers everyone whose lives it touches—and carries them far beyond the immediate impact to the possible impacts on the world for generations to come. The eighth house asks you to consider how your project or vision in some way helps to create something better for those who come after you. Your project must be sustainable. Either it must be able to sustain itself or you must put some system in place to support those to come in sustaining it. This house asks you to look at the impact of your project, not just on your direct descendants, but on the descendants of your community, and then of your generation.

Most people would say that their goals in life are to live fully, be successful, and be happy. Other than perhaps providing for their children and grandchildren, many people don't give a lot of thought to their responsibilities for the world's future or for leaving the world better for having been here. When they do think about their legacy, it is usually in terms of material possessions, contributions, or fame. While those contributions may be significant, the idea of a legacy also includes ways of thinking, believing, and being in the world. I call this your "energetic legacy." Your thoughts, beliefs, intentions, and presence of being are all energy and, as you know from the mirror metaphor of the holographic universe, who you are and what you think and believe is constantly broadcast throughout the mass consciousness. It is the combination of everyone's thoughts, intentions, beliefs, and actions that creates that mass consciousness. When thought, intention, belief, and action are focused and aligned among a group of people, a very small percentage of a population—less than one percent—can have a significant impact on the mass consciousness.

Your thoughts go out into the universe as vibrations. Each word you speak has an impact on the energy around you. Every action you take either reinforces the energy patterns that are already in place or helps shift them to something new. Your choices for the present not only create your future;

they contribute to the consciousness into which future genera-tions are born. This is the true essence of the eighth house: raising your individual consciousness for the benefit of future generations.

It is in the context of this larger legacy that you consider your project or vision in this last house. This house calls you to the long-term view—to an awareness of the potential impact of your project, not just for the next few months or years, but for the next few generations. It also reminds you to remain aware of the greater legacy being created by how you live, even while focusing on a specific project or vision.

Before continuing, take time to journal about the following questions:

• What is the energetic legacy you are creating through this project? What beliefs, expectations, thoughts, and pres-ence does it broadcast? What does it contribute to the mass consciousness?

• How does your project or vision contribute to generations to come?

• What is the energetic legacy you are creating through how you live your life? How are you contributing to the raising of human consciousness?

The eighth house also calls you to consider your past. It invites you to look at your family heritage and cultural tradi-tions and ask: What do I feel called to perpetuate? Perhaps you feel a deep desire to honor and sustain certain traditions, beliefs, practices, or values. There may be aspects of your her-itage to which you feel a strong allegiance and a desire to carry them forward in history. You may also feel that aspects of your heritage have run their course, yet need to be remembered and honored for their importance in their own time.

On the other hand, you may feel called to change some aspects of your heritage or culture—certain beliefs, practices, or traditions that stand in the way of progressive growth and development. It is each generation's responsibility to free future generations from limiting beliefs and traditions. The eighth house calls your awareness to these limiting beliefs and traditions so you can consider how your project contributes to a new legacy.

Consider these questions:

- What traditions, beliefs, practices, and/or values do you feel called to carry into the future?

- How can your project or vision be a vehicle for them?

- What are the limiting beliefs, traditions, or values that you feel called to change so that future generations are born into a different consciousness?

- How does your project or vision help facilitate this new energetic legacy?

If you have never considered your life and goals from this universal perspective, these questions may seem overwhelming. You may only have considered your project or vision within the context of your personal life or your family, community, or organization. Your current project may not feel as significant in the big scheme of things. Not so. Regardless of the scope or magnitude of your current vision, it is still an energy system that reaches out to the universe and spreads its vibration. Its potential carries an energetic vibration and, through choosing to partner with that potential to bring it into form, you broadcast a strong energetic signal to the universe of all that your project represents. You call forth that potential, not just for your life, but for the world.

Linear and Simultaneous Space/Time

In the seventh house, the highway metaphor illustrated how you can easily move back and forth between linear and simultaneous time/space. That same metaphor can illuminate your relationship to the past and future. The lanes that you and those who have gone before you chose to travel have brought you to this moment in time and space. Different choices in the past would have led to a different present. The lane in which you choose to travel in the present determines what your future will be. In the present moment, the future has many possibilities. When you choose a particular lane, you increase the chances of a particular outcome or future happening. If you change lanes, you shift the odds toward a different future. Every choice you make in the present determines some aspect of your future, whether that choice is a belief, an attitude, a decision, or an action.

Visit the simultaneous time/space highway again in the following exercise.

Exercise 17: Seeing the Bigger Perspective

Settle into your Point of Stillness, then return to the timeline highway. Float high above the highway so that you can once again see or perceive the past, present, and future all happening simultaneously. Locate your project and the lane that led to it in the future. From this perspective, consider the following questions:

- Where are you headed in your life as a result of this project? Where does this lane go as it continues beyond your project?

- Is this the lane you want to travel in? Is it taking you to the next destination you choose for your life, as well as the next destination you choose for your family, community, and the world?

- Is the lane in which you are traveling leading to a future that will serve generations to come?

- What if you made all decisions and choices as if you were making them for a whole community of people? What if you considered every decision as if you were making that choice for a nation or a multi-national corporation? Would you make the same choice? Would the aim of your project be the same if it were a part of a national or global initiative?

After considering these questions, return your awareness to the present moment, bringing with you the wisdom you have gathered from the timeline highway. What new perspective do you now have on your project, its manifestation process, and the importance of it being fully manifested?

Obviously, most of our individual projects do not play out on a national or global stage. Even if they don't directly impact many people, however, what is their energetic legacy? Regardless of a project's scope or magnitude, its energy is still being broadcast to the mass consciousness and contributing a particular vibrational frequency to that consciousness.

Through these considerations, the eighth house calls you to fully accept your responsibility as a co-creator of our collective present and future. Your every thought, word, and action are a part of that creative process. Your words, thoughts, and actions shape your present and your future—not just for you individually, but for the entire global family.

As you leave this final house of the Manifestation Wheel, consider the following questions:

- Is your project sustainable? Can you sustain it, and can it sustain you—emotionally, physically, mentally, and spiritually?

- How conscious are you of how your thoughts, intentions, beliefs, words, and actions impact future generations? How are you doing your part to create a positive future for all those to come, not just your direct descendants?

- House #1 Check-in: When you look at your project within the context of legacy, do you see it any differently? Is there anything about your project that needs to change?

- House #2 Check-in: Has considering legacy in any way compromised your sense of inner peace? If so, what needs to shift?

- House #3 Check-in: In the context of legacy, do you have more or less enthusiasm and motivation for your project? If less, what needs to shift?

- House #4 Check-in: How has looking at your project from the perspective of legacy impacted your thoughts about the future? Does anything need to shift within your project? Within your life?

- House #5 Check-in: Through your work in this house, do you continue to see how your vision will nurture and add value to your life and the lives of others, both now and in the future?

- House #6 Check-in: As you continue to expand your awareness, does your action plan need any adjustment? If so, what adjustments need to be made?

- House #7 Check-in: What more have you discovered about living intuitively after your work in the eighth house? What more do you understand about being in command of the manifestation process and dancing with all of your co-creative partners, including Consciousness and potential?

Congratulations! You have made it all the way around the Manifestation Wheel. Your project or vision should be well on its way to full manifestation. It may have already happened. The eighth house takes you right back to the first house, where you once again consider where you are, what your intentions are now, and then begin your next project or the next phase of this current one. If you are working on a new phase of the same project, your subsequent trips around the Wheel will go much more quickly. You have done the big work now. Your continued work with the Wheel will just be a matter of tweaking things to keep the energies aligned and flowing. If you are putting a new project on the Wheel, it, too, will most likely move around the Wheel more quickly. As, with each successive project, you bring all of your life into increasing alignment, the manifestation becomes easier.

CHAPTER 11

The Manifestation Wheel in Your Personal Life

It is when we go beyond our edge that we discover
the next layer of potential, experience ourselves
and our relationship to the world in a new way, and
find new meaning to the concept of possibility.

Now that you have learned the essence of each house of the
Manifestation Wheel, let your intuition guide you as you take
your projects around it. The questions below can support you
in the process and help you focus on the essence of each house.
However, don't feel limited to these questions. You may also
find that every question does not need to be answered. Let your
intuition guide you to the questions that are relevant to your
specific project. As you become more familiar with the Wheel,
the energy of each house may serve you more powerfully than
the specific questions presented here. The Wheel is a dynamic
energetic tool. Tap into its essence. Let the manifestation
process itself, the potential waiting to emerge through your
project, and the greater Consciousness all become your co-
creative partners.

House #1: Intention

- What is the project, goal, desire, or vision you are putting on the Wheel?

- What is the greatest potential of this project or vision? What wants to happen?

- What are the characteristics of the person who would fully manifest that potential?

Create your statement of intention by supplying the following information:

Project/Vision/Goal:

Potential:

Commitment:

House #2: Peace

- What is your "gut feeling" when you think about your manifestation project or vision? Are you at peace with it?

- Are you ready to accept the full manifestation of your vision? How will your life be different? How does that feel?

- Are you pursuing any part of your project because you think you "should" or because someone else thinks you should? If so, is this what really wants to happen?

- What, if any, unfulfilled dreams or aspirations must you release or harmonize in order to be free of the past and move forward with this project?

- Are there any hidden agendas related to your project?

- What is your relationship to the world around you? Are there conflicts that need to be resolved? If so, how can you resolve them?

- House #1 Check-in: After your work in the second house, what if any revisions must you make to your intention and commitments of the first house? How do you see the potential of your project or vision differently?

House #3: Energy

- What will you be, do, and/or have that is different from your current situation once you have manifested your vision?

- Why do you want this? Why is it important to you?

- On a scale of one to ten, ten being the highest, what is your level of passion and excitement for this project?

- What must you give up, even temporarily, to manifest this vision? Activities, material things, habits, relationships, responsibilities, thoughts, beliefs? Are you willing to do that?

- What are you willing to risk to manifest this vision? How much risk is acceptable? How much is too much?

- What do you risk by *not* manifesting this vision?

- Are you willing to invest time and money in this manifestation project? If so, how much?

- What must happen to build a sense of momentum and energy focus toward this vision?

- What does your current reality field feel like? Does it fully serve the manifestation of your project? If not, what new reality field will you create?

- House #1 Check-in: Does your work in the third house reinforce your intention and commitments, or cause you to question them? What, if anything, needs to shift in your intention and commitments?

- House #2 Check-in: Does your work in the third house in any way compromise your sense of peace around the manifestation of your vision? If so, what needs to shift?

House #4: Guidance

Take time to remember the future—a time after your project has been completed or your vision manifested. Then consider the following questions:

- Having visited the future, what more do you now know about your project, its potential and possibilities, and the road ahead?

- What, if any, thought patterns, habits, or beliefs need to shift to best facilitate the manifestation of your vision? How can you make those shifts?

- What is your level of patience regarding this project? Have you achieved a balance between being patient enough and putting off moving forward?

- House #1 Check-in: Having visited the future, how has your understanding of your project or vision shifted?

What, if any, revisions need to be made in your intention or your commitments?

- House #2 Check-in: Having visited the future, is your sense of peace compromised in any way? If so, what needs to shift?

- House #3 Check-in: Does visiting the future create more or less enthusiasm and motivation for your project? If less, what needs to shift?

House #5: Empowerment

- What is the message that people are getting about you and your project as you manifest this vision? Is this the message you want them to receive?

- How does the manifestation of your vision serve you directly? What are its gifts?

- How does the manifestation of your vision serve others? What are its gifts for them?

- As you consider your role in this manifestation process, is it a role you want to play? Is this how you want to be seen by others?

- Does playing this role enrich your life, or is it costing you in some way?

- Does your playing this role help others to be all that they can be?

- How does your project call you to be all that you can be? How does it challenge you to grow in positive and constructive ways?

- How does your project call everyone involved to be all they can be? How does it challenge them to grow in positive and constructive ways?

- Do you like who you are becoming as you pursue this project?

- As you look at others involved in your project, do you like who they are becoming through it?

- Is there any way in which your project manipulates anyone, including yourself, to be someone they are not?

- Is there anything about this project or its process that could cause harm to anyone?

- What leadership skills or characteristics do you need to develop or refine in order to accomplish your goal?

- House #1 Check-in: How does your work in this house help you see and commit to your vision more clearly?

- House #2 Check-in: After your work in this house, has your sense of peace around the manifestation of your vision been compromised in any way? If so, what needs to shift?

- House #3 Check-in: After your work in this house, do you feel more or less enthusiasm and motivation for the accomplishment of your vision? If less, what needs to shift?

- House #4 Check-in: After your work in this house, do you see your future any differently? If so, how is it guiding you? Does anything need to shift?

House #6: Action

Follow the process for creating an action plan on pages 115–120. Then check in with the previous houses:

- House #1 Check-in: Having created an action plan, has anything shifted in your understanding of your vision or project? What, if anything, needs to change in your intention and/or commitment?

- House #2 Check-in: Does your action plan in any way compromise your sense of inner peace? If so, what needs to shift?

- House #3 Check-in: Does your action plan create more or less enthusiasm and motivation for your project? If less, what needs to shift?

- House #4 Check-in: Is your action plan in harmony with what you have seen of the future? If not, what needs to shift?

- House #5 Check-in: How does the implementation of your action plan continue to nurture, empower, and add value to your life and to the lives of others?

House #7: Surrender

- How does your vision or project fit into the larger context of your life? How does it relate to your ongoing journey?

- How does your vision or project relate to your soul mission or life purpose?

- To what must you surrender in order to more fully realize your greatest potential?

- When you tap into "what wants to happen" for the greater good, how does your project fit into that context? To what universal potential are you being asked to surrender?

- Are you making time and space for regular meditation, introspection, and reflection? Are you engaging in on-going intuitive conversation with your soul, Consciousness, and the potential of your project? If so, what does that feel like? If not, how can you get started?

- Are you surrendering your vision to the unseen forces to allow synergy and synchronicity to occur? If so, what are you experiencing? If not, what will help you fully surrender? How can that happen?

- House #1 Check-in: What, if anything, has shifted in your intention and personal commitments as a result of surrendering to your project and its momentum and to the universal potential of this time?

- House #2 Check-in: Has your work in the seventh house in any way compromised your sense of inner peace? If so, what needs to shift?

- House #3 Check-in: Do you have more or less enthusiasm and motivation for your project after your work in the seventh house? If less, what needs to shift?

- House #4 Check-in: How has your work in this house impacted your vision of the future? Does anything need to shift?

- House #5 Check-in: Through your work in this house, do you continue to see how your project will nurture and add value to your life and the lives of others?

- House #6 Check-in: As you surrender on deeper and higher levels, what, if any, adjustments are called for in your action plan?

House #8: Legacy

- What is the energetic legacy you are creating through your project? What beliefs, expectations, thoughts, and presence are you broadcasting? What are you contributing to the mass consciousness?

- How does your project or vision contribute to generations to come?

- How can your project or vision be a vehicle for the traditions, beliefs, practices, and/or values you feel called to carry into the future?

- How does your project or vision help change limiting beliefs, traditions, or values from your heritage and facilitate a new energetic legacy?

- Where are you headed in your life as a result of this project?

- How, if at all, would you change your decisions and choices regarding this project if they were impacting a whole community, a nation, or a multi-national corporation? Would you make the same choices? Would the aim of your project be the same if it were a part of a national or global initiative?

- House #1 Check-in: When you look at your project within the context of legacy, do you see it any differently? Is there anything about your project that needs to change in order to create the legacy you desire?

- House #2 Check-in: Has considering legacy in any way compromised your sense of inner peace? If so, what needs to shift?

- House #3 Check-in: In the context of legacy, do you have more or less enthusiasm and motivation for your project? If less, what needs to shift?

- House #4 Check-in: How has looking at your project from the perspective of legacy impacted your thoughts about the future? What, if anything, needs to shift within your project or your life?

- House #5 Check-in: Through your work in this house, do you continue to see how your vision will nurture and add value to your life and the lives of others, now and in the future?

- House #6 Check-in: As you expand your awareness, what, if any, adjustments need to be made to your action plan?

- House #7 Check-in: What has your work in the eighth house taught you about living intuitively? What have you learned about being in command of the manifestation process and dancing with all of your co-creative partners, including Consciousness and potential?

CHAPTER 12

The Manifestation Wheel in Your Organization or Business

In the big picture view, business and organizational structures are here to serve the ongoing evolution of society and culture. The concepts of manifestation open the door to new levels of engagement in commerce and community, and a future that we have only begun to imagine.

The Manifestation Wheel is a powerful tool for strategic planning, project development and management, and visioning and team building in organizational or business structures. Now that you understand the essence of each house, focus on that essence and let your intuition guide you as you recognize the questions and concepts you must address for your particular project. Refer back to the exercises and processes for each house and adapt them as needed for your team, group, or organization.

House #1: Intention

The first house calls you and your team to clarify the core mission and potential of your project, and then to commit to that mission and potential and the manifestation process. This house calls you to change and grow, to stretch beyond your comfort zone for personal and professional development. Here, you commit to facing fears, re-evaluating beliefs and behaviors, and letting go of assumptions. The important steps taken in this house are:

- Clarify the mission and potential of your project.

- Clarify the intention of your vision and how it relates to the mission and potential of your team or organization.

- Commit to and accept your responsibility in the manifestation process.

- Discipline your thoughts and make the necessary paradigm shifts that allow your project to manifest.

As you work in the first house, ask your group or team these key questions:

- What is the vision/project we are putting on the Wheel?

- What is the core mission and potential of our project? What wants to happen?

- Have we fully claimed this mission and are we committed to living and working according to it in daily work life? If not, how can we take that step?

- What are the characteristics of an organization and its members that would fully manifest that potential?

- Who do we commit to being as an organization and as individuals through this manifestation process?

- Are we ready and willing to take full responsibility for our roles, individually and as a team, in the co-creative process of manifesting this vision?

Create your statement of intention by supplying the following information:

Project/Vision/Goal:

Potential:

Commitment:

House #2: Peace

In the first house, you establish clear intention; in the second house, you make peace with the intention, your project, and its ultimate outcome. The important steps taken in this house are:

- Resolve conflicts, face fears, dissolve resistance.

- Make peace with your intention, its potential, and the possible outcomes.

- Release the past.

- Ensure that your project is in harmony with both organizational and personal values.

As you work in the second house, ask your group or team these key questions:

- What is our "gut reaction" when we look at or think about our project? Is the project in complete harmony with the mission and potential of the team? Of the company or organization? Are we at peace with this project?

- Are we pursuing any part of our project because we think we "should" or because someone else thinks we should? If so, is this what really wants to happen?

- What, if any, unfulfilled business or organizational aspirations or dreams must we release or harmonize in order to move forward with this project?

- Are there any hidden agendas among team members or from another part of the organization that impact our project?

- What is our organization's relationship to its community and the world? Are there conflicts that need to be resolved? If so, how can we resolve them?

- What needs to shift in order for inner peace to be a way of life for our organization? What is one step we can take today?

- House #1 Check-in: After our work in the second house, what if any revisions need to be made to our intention and commitments of the first house? How do we see the potential of our project or vision differently?

House #3: Energy

In the third house, you generate passion and energy around your vision/project and are inspired by its potential. At this stage, you begin to do research. You identify the skills, tools, and resources that will be necessary for manifestation and begin gathering and developing them. Finally, you create an intentional reality field for your project. The important steps taken in this house are:

- Generate passion and energy for the project.

- Mastermind possible steps and goals.

- Identify resources and alliances.

- Create reality fields.

    Begin by masterminding your project.

Exercise 18: Masterminding a Group Project

Go to your Point of Stillness. If team members have learned to do this on their own, allow a few moments for everyone to settle in. If not, use the Point of Stillness exercise on page 31 as a script to guide them through the process.

Once everyone is settled, ask them to imagine the greatest potential of your project or vision floating out in the middle of the group or in front of the room. Just have fun with this, and acknowledge that everyone's experience will be different. Some will "see" it; others will "feel" it; some may "hear" it. Give everyone a chance to speak about whatever they perceive. Make no judgments or criticisms about anyone's observations. This must be a space where everyone feels completely free to share absolutely anything about what they perceive, whether it is simply a color, a feeling, or a long and involved message.

Sense the level of energy, motivation, and passion present for the project. Is the energy and motivation high? Is there passion for your project? If yes, mastermind how best to harness that energy and passion. If no, mastermind how best to get the energy and motivation moving! There has to be passion and personal motivation from all involved to steward the greatest potential.

This part of your masterminding session may last a few minutes or, if ideas are starting to fly, for quite a while. Just follow the energy, remain aware of what wants to happen next, and when it is time, move on.

Ask open questions to facilitate your masterminding session. Assign someone to take notes on everything that transpires. Accept every idea, thought, or inspiration. Now is not the time to analyze or decide whether something is a good idea or whether or not it will work. That will block the energy. This process is pure inspiration and intuition. Encourage everyone to speak freely, even if they don't fully understand what they are saying. Some questions you can consider are:

- What goals may we consider as steps toward manifestation?

- What resources, including time, money, and expertise, must be attracted?

- What alliances would be helpful?

- Is there space, time, and energy in this organization for this manifestation, or are things too crowded? If there is no room, how can we open up more space, time, and energy to make room for this project?

Follow the energy until it feels as if the masterminding session is over. Before you leave the session, take a moment to ask participants about their experience. Do they feel different now about the project and its manifestation? What do they now know about the project that they didn't know before? And most important, ask everyone to notice how they did what they just did. Intuitive work is much simpler than we often make it out to be. Chances are all they did was to get out of their own way intellectually and let it happen. How can this work even better the next time?

Many of the ideas that come out of this session will become a part of the action plan you create in the sixth house. Keep the notes from this session in a safe place so you can refer to them later.

As you work in the third house, ask your group or team these key questions:

- How will our organization and its members be different once the vision is manifested? How will we feel and do things differently, and what will we have that we do not have now?

- Why do we want this? Why is it important to us and to the organization?

- On a scale of one to ten, ten being the highest, what is the level of passion and excitement for this project, within our group and in the organization as a whole?

- What must we give up or sacrifice, even temporarily, to manifest this vision? Activities, material things, practices, commitments, habits, associations, thoughts, beliefs?

- Are we willing to do that? Can our organization afford to give this up? Can we afford not to?

- What do we risk by not manifesting this vision?

- How much time and money is the organization willing to invest in this manifestation project?

- What goals may we consider as steps toward manifestation?

- What resources, including time, money, and expertise, must be attracted?

- What alliances would be helpful?

- Are these resources and alliances readily available, or must we find or create them?

- What needs to happen to build a sense of momentum and energy focus toward this vision?

- What does our current reality field feel like? Does it fully serve the manifestation of this project? If not, what new reality field will we create?

- House #1 Check-in: Does our work in the third house reinforce our intention and commitments, or cause us to question them? What, if anything, needs to shift in our intention and commitments?

- House #2 Check-in: Does our work in the third house in any way compromise our sense of peace around the manifestation of our vision? If so, what needs to shift?

House #4: Guidance

In the fourth house, you step out of "creative" mode and into "reflective" mode, letting your intuition give you an even clearer and more expanded picture of what things can look like when you complete your project. The important steps taken in this house are:

- Tap into your intuition and the quantum field as a source of guidance and inspiration for the completion of the project.

- Learn to remember the future.

  Begin by taking a trip on the Potential Expressway.

Exercise 19: Traveling the Potential Expressway with a Group

This exercise is best done in an open indoor or outdoor space where everyone can move around. Let one person facilitate the exercise and guide the rest of the group through the process.

Choose a spot to represent this present time in your organization and ask everyone to stand there. Take a few moments before you begin for everyone to reinforce the reality field you have created and to strengthen the embodiment of your project and its greatest potential. Then read through the following script slowly to allow your group members to experience what is presented.

Let go of any pre-conceived ideas or expectations about what you should experience or discover. Close your eyes and imagine our group on the Potential Expressway, a magical highway whose lanes can take us anywhere in time or space. The entire expressway is reserved for us right now; there is no one else on it except us and those who may be a part of our future, so we can take our time and not worry about holding up traffic.

We can travel this expressway using any mode of transportation—a sports car, a limousine, a speedboat or a yacht, a bicycle or private jet, walking or even hitchhiking. How do you imagine our group will travel? Have fun with this and let your intuition show you the best vehicle for our journey.

As we travel down the expressway, the lanes begin to diverge, each going in a different direction. You may see signs telling you where the different lanes are going; you may not. Trust that you will know what each possible outcome is when you arrive there. Choose a lane for our group to travel, open your eyes, and move to a spot that you choose to represent your first possible outcome. Chances are people will move to different places. That's fine. Just go where your intuition leads you. [Allow time for them to move.] Now, standing in the energy of this outcome, consider the following questions:

- *What is this outcome? Describe it.*

- *Tune into the energy of this possibility. How does it feel?*

- *Who do we as an organization become here?*

- *What are the benefits of this particular outcome?*

- *What is the date now that our project is complete and this outcome is realized?*

- *Was the journey to this outcome easy or challenging?*

- *Is there anything about this outcome that doesn't feel right to you?*

- *On a scale of one to ten, with ten being the best, how would you rate this outcome?*

Stay with your feeling and intuition; resist the temptation to figure things out or analyze them. Just take what comes.

Open your eyes and go back to your starting place. Now close them again and imagine yourself on the Potential Expressway with all the lanes running side by side. Choose another lane and follow it as it diverges from the others and heads to its specific outcome. Perhaps you'll see a sign along the way telling you where you are headed; perhaps you won't. When you are ready, open your eyes and move to a different spot that you choose to represent this possible outcome. Again, don't worry if everyone goes to a different spot. [Give them time to move. Then ask each of the above questions again.]

Repeat this process until the group has visited several possible outcomes, answered the questions there, and felt the energy of each one. Then ask everyone to return to the starting place and reflect on all of the possible outcomes. Give each person a chance to share the outcomes they discovered and how they felt. Assign someone to make notes about the various outcomes presented by group members. Then ask the group to select several outcomes that seem the most promising or hold the most energy. You may then want to ask them to stand in the spot of these possible outcomes and compare how they feel. Rate them on a scale of one to ten. Which one do they rate the highest? Which one does the group's intuition tell them is the outcome to choose because it just feels right?

As a group, choose the outcome you want to focus on as you continue in the manifestation process, then go back to the spot that represents that outcome. Breathe in your chosen outcome. Feel its energy and embody it. What is the realty field that is automatically created when you embody that energy? Memorize it. Lock in that feeling.

Now you are ready to embody the future of your outcome and reinforce its reality field. Ask everyone to stand with enough space around them so they can take a step forward. Reading slowly, guide them with the following script:

Close your eyes and take a few moments to settle into your Point of Stillness. Imagine in front of you a movie of some point in the future when our project is fully manifested. Look into the picture and feel its energy. Notice who is there. Notice what sounds you hear. How would you describe our group in that picture? How would you describe yourself there? Does what you perceive of the future feel good or right to you? Is it what we as a group say we want? If not, what needs to change in our intention? What would make it feel right to you? Make the necessary adjustments.

When what you see and feel is what you want, step into the movie and begin living it. Embody the energy and vibrational frequency. Check to make sure that everything feels right to you, then describe the reality field. Is it the same as the reality field we created in the third house or is it different? If different, which reality field will best serve the manifestation of our vision?

As you embody the energy of our vision now fully manifested, what do you know about what must be the focus of our thought and action for the next six months? What must be the focus of our thought and action for the next month? The next week? For the rest of today?

Take time for each person to share their discoveries and thoughts. Assign a scribe to record it all, as it will help you when you create your action plan in the sixth house.

As you conclude your work in the fourth house, ask your group or team these key questions:

- Having visited the future, what more do we know now about our project, its potential and possibilities, and the road ahead?

- What thought patterns, habits, or beliefs need to shift within our team and/or organization to best facilitate the manifestation of our vision? How can we make those shifts?

- What is our level of patience regarding this project? Is there a balance between being patient enough and putting off moving forward?

- What new responsibilities must we now accept, as individuals and as a team, to manifest these expanded possibilities of the future?

- House #1 Check-in: Having visited the future, how has our understanding of our project or vision shifted? What, if any, revisions must we make in our intention or commitments?

- House #2 Check-in: Having visited the future, is our sense of peace compromised in any way? If so, what needs to shift?

- House #3 Check-in: Does visiting the future create more or less enthusiasm and motivation for our project? If less, what needs to shift?

House #5: Empowerment

In the fifth house, you nurture relationships and empower individuals as leaders. Here, you consider how your project will influence the lives of everyone involved in it, as well as those it will impact, consciously and unconsciously. You consider how it will affect the company and all the businesses, people, and environments it will touch. In the fifth house, you define your team's and your project's role in building community and learn how everything is a part of a greater whole. Everything impacts everything else. The important steps taken in this house are:

- Consider the impact of your project within the context of community.

- Call forth the best from everyone involved in the project.

- Assess and step into the leadership required for this project.

As you work in the fifth house, ask your group or team these key questions:

- What is the message that people are getting about us and this project as it manifests? Is this the message we want them to receive?

- How does the manifestation of our vision serve this organization directly? What are its gifts?

- How does it serve others?

- As we consider our roles in this manifestation process, both individually and collectively, are these roles we want to play?

- How does our project call all team members to be all that they can be? How does it challenge them to grow in positive and constructive ways?

- How does our project call others who are involved to be all that they can be? How does it challenge them to grow in positive and constructive ways?

- Do we like who we are becoming as an organization and as individuals as we pursue this project?

- Do we like who others involved in the project are becoming through this process?

- Is there any way in which our project manipulates anyone or any other organization to be someone or something they are not?

- Is there anything about our project or its process that can cause harm to anyone or any other group or organization?

- What leadership skills or characteristics do we need to develop or refine, either as individuals or as an organization, to accomplish our goal?

- House #1 Check-in: How does our work in this house help us see and commit to our vision more clearly?

- House #2 Check-in: After our work in this house, has our sense of peace around the manifestation of our vision been compromised in any way? If so, what needs to shift?

- House #3 Check-in: After our work in this house, do we feel more or less enthusiasm and motivation for the accomplishment of our vision? If less, what needs to shift?

- House #4 Check-in: After our work in this house, do we see our future any differently? If so, how is it guiding us?

House #6: Action

In the sixth house, you make a detailed action plan by bringing together what you intuitively and intellectually know needs to be done and actually doing it. The important steps taken in this house are:

- Create an initial action plan.

- Implement the plan.

Follow the process for creating an action plan on pages 115–120. Your entire group can go through the process together. Assign one person to facilitate the process and another to be the scribe. After you have completed your action plan map, check in with the previous houses:

- House #1 Check-in: Having created an action plan, has anything shifted in our understanding of this vision or project? What, if anything, needs to change in our intention and/or commitment?

- House #2 Check-in: Does this action plan in any way compromise our sense of inner peace? If so, what needs to shift?

- House #3 Check-in: Does this action plan create more or less enthusiasm and motivation for our project? If less, what needs to shift?

- House #4 Check-in: Is our action plan in harmony with what we have seen of the future? If not, what needs to shift?

- House #5 Check-in: How does the implementation of our action plan nurture, empower, and add value to our lives and to the lives of others?

House #7: Surrender

In the seventh house, you let go, give up control, and enter a new phase of working intuitively with Consciousness and the project's potential for support and guidance. Living intuitively means surrendering your rational mind to the larger intuitive mind, and stepping out of a process that is limited to "thinking," and into one that involves all of your inner and outer senses. It means "intuiting" life. The important steps taken in this house are:

- Surrender to the manifestation process.

- Work intuitively.

- Trust that your project will go where it needs to go.

- Expect synergy and synchronicity as a natural way of organizational and business reality and practice.

- Follow the energy of your project as it manifests.

As you work in the seventh house, ask your group or team these key questions:

- How does our vision or project fit into the larger context of our organization and its ongoing growth and development?

- How does our vision or project relate to our organization's soul mission or purpose?

- To what must we, as a team, surrender in order to more fully realize our greatest potential?

- When we tap into "what wants to happen" for the greater good, how does our project fit into that context? To what universal potential are we being asked to surrender?

- As a team, how are we engaging in an ongoing intuitive conversation with the soul of our organization, Consciousness, and the potential of our project?

- Are we surrendering our vision to the unseen forces to allow synergy and synchronicity to occur? If so, what are we experiencing? If not, what must we do to fully surrender? How can that happen?

- House #1 Check-in: What, if anything, has shifted in our intention and commitments as a result of surrendering to our project and its momentum, and to the universal potential of this time?

- House #2 Check-in: Has our work in the seventh house in any way compromised our sense of inner peace? If so, what needs to shift?

- House #3 Check-in: Do we have more or less enthusiasm and motivation for our project after our work in the seventh house? If less, what needs to shift?

- House #4 Check-in: How has our work in this house impacted our vision of the future? Does anything need to shift?

- House #5 Check-in: Through our work in this house, do we continue to see how our project will nurture and add value to our organization and to the larger community?

- House #6 Check-in: As we surrender on deeper and higher levels, what, if any, adjustments are called for in our action plan?

House #8: Legacy

In the eighth and final house, your view of your vision/project expands to a global perspective. Here, you consider your project within the context of legacy. The eighth house calls you to feel the interconnectedness of all people and the environment, and to do business or run your organization in such a way that it contributes to, honors, and sustains life for all generations to come. The important steps taken in this house are:

- Consider the legacy being created by your project and by your organization.

- Consider the sustainability of your project for your organization, its members, and future generations.

As you work in the eighth house, ask your group or team these key questions:

- Is our project sustainable? Can we sustain it, and can it sustain us on multiple levels: physically, emotionally, mentally, and spiritually?

- What is the energetic legacy our organization is creating through this project? What beliefs, expectations, thoughts, and presence are we broadcasting? What are we contributing to the mass consciousness?

- How is our project or vision contributing to generations to come?

- What traditions, beliefs, practices, and/or values does our organization feel called to carry into the future?

- How can our project or vision be a vehicle for them?

- What are the limiting beliefs, practices, or values that our organization feels called to change so that future generations are born into a different consciousness?

- How does our project or vision help facilitate this new energetic legacy?

- Where are we headed as an organization and as team members as a result of this project?

- How conscious are we of how our thoughts, intentions, beliefs, words, and actions as an organization impact future generations? How are we doing our part to create a positive future for all those to come?

- House #1 Check-in: When we look at our project within the context of legacy, do we see it any differently? Is there anything about our project that needs to change to create the legacy we desire?

- House #2 Check-in: Has considering legacy in any way compromised our sense of inner peace? If so, what needs to shift?

- House #3 Check-in: In the context of legacy, do we have more or less enthusiasm and motivation for our project? If less, what needs to shift?

- House #4 Check-in: How has looking at our project from the perspective of legacy impacted our thoughts about the future? What, if anything, needs to shift within our project or organization?

- House #5 Check-in: Through our work in this house, do we continue to see how our vision will nurture and add value to our lives and the lives of others, now and in the future?

- House #6 Check-in: As we continue to expand our awareness, what, if any, adjustments do we need to make to our action plan?

- House #7 Check-in: What have we discovered about working intuitively as a team or an organization in our work in the eighth house? What more do we understand about being in command of the manifestation process and dancing with all of our co-creative partners, including Consciousness and potential?

Manifestation as a Way of Life

Congratulations on completing your journey around the Manifestation Wheel. You have learned how to use a very powerful tool that can serve you in every aspect of your life. I encourage you to begin another trip around the Wheel as soon as you finish your first project—either the next phase of your first project or something completely new. Taking a second trip around the Wheel immediately can help you internalize the manifestation process.

As you apply the Wheel to various dreams and projects in your life, you may end up working on several projects at once on several different Wheels. When you have a major manifestation project that spans weeks, months, or even years, it is good practice to give each aspect or component of the project its own Wheel. Have a master Wheel for the overall project and as many Wheels within it as you need for the project's individual components. This ensures that the energy remains aligned at all levels of the project.

As you become more facile with the Manifestation Wheel, you will intuitively discover more about each house. The Wheel will continue to come alive for you in unique ways. This is part of its power. Ultimately, the specific questions you ask and the exercises you do are not as important as the energetic essence of each house. That energetic essence may show up differently for each project. You can even begin your work in each house by asking: What is the greatest potential wanting to happen for my project in this house? Your goal is to work with the greatest potential of your project or vision, and tap into what wants to happen in each house. When you have become skilled enough to work the Wheel on this level of intuition and awareness, you are truly on your way to manifestation mastery.

As you have probably realized, however, the Manifestation Wheel is about much more than accomplishing a goal or manifesting a vision. It is about life alignment, higher perspective, and living in harmony with the world around you and the world as a whole. Through the Wheel, you gain a better understanding of how you fit into the world—in the larger scheme of things and in the daily living of your soul's purpose. In addition, you discover greater potential in your project or your life than you previously imagined.

We have worked with the Manifestation Wheel as a two-dimensional model. Now that you know the concepts and principles of the Wheel, you can explore it in its three-dimensional form—a spiral. Imagine the Wheel as a spiral staircase whose center pole is your essence, your soul, and its mission—your overall reason for being. Your soul, its mission, and your personal potential are the pivot on which the spiral turns.

In the Manifestation Spiral, you enter the House of Intention at the ground level and, with each successive house, ascend one step higher. Each successive step of the spiral is wider than the previous one, so the outer edge of the staircase forms a constantly expanding circle. With each house and each successively higher and wider step, your awareness of your project or vision, and of who you are within it and within the world, expands.

To expand on the metaphor, it's as if the eight houses take you from one level of awareness to the next. As you return from the eighth house to the first, instead of starting over at the ground level, you step up into the next level of awareness. Each time you return to the first house, you ascend to a new level of "beingness" in the world.

As you climb higher on the Manifestation Spiral, you become, in effect, the whole spiral. You become aware of every level at once, living the principles and concepts of all the houses at the same time, living manifestation in every moment. Manifestation simply becomes your way of life. The more trips you make around the Spiral, the more it becomes a part of you and you a part of it. Your instinct is to bring all thoughts, intentions, beliefs, choices, decisions, and actions into alignment. All eight houses become present in every step you take. The Manifestation Spiral becomes a constantly spinning overlay for your life. Every day, from the most mundane to the grandest creations of your life, you live its principles.

Your ultimate goal in working with the Manifestation Wheel is to make your life a constant flow of manifestation of the greatest potential in every moment, situation, or circumstance. You think it; it appears—maybe not immediately, but, given the time it needs, it will unfold. Manifestation is just the way you live. It's what is normal. To others, it appears that you lead a charmed life. However, you know that you have mastered the art and technology of co-creation and that everything that happens, at least within the context of unfolding potential, is somewhat predictable.

Mastering manifestation as the art of co-creation is a huge gift—a gift to yourself of living in harmony with the universe and with Consciousness in extraordinary ways; a gift to the world because you live every day in that incredible harmony. In so doing, you model this extraordinary way of living for others, serving the world through your abilities to manifest good for all.

This gift is available to everyone. It just requires discipline, focus, and commitment. Michelangelo's words are as appropriate here as they were at the beginning of our journey around the Wheel: "The greatest danger for most of us is not that our aim is too high and we miss it, but that it is too low and we reach it." Take the time to discipline your thoughts, focus your energy, and commit to manifestation mastery. Let the Manifestation Wheel take you to heights you never imagined possible. Live its principles and potential, and you will manifest wonderful gifts for yourself and for the world.

BIBLIOGRAPHY

Braden, Gregg. *Awakening to Zero Point*. Bellevue, WA: Radio Bookstore Press, 1997.

———. *The Isaiah Effect*. New York: Three Rivers Press, 2000.

———. *The Divine Matrix: Bridging Time, Space, Miracles, and Belief*. Carlsbad, CA: Hay House, 2007.

Capra, Fritjof. *The Tao of Physics*. Boston: Shambhala, 2000.

Childre, Doc and Howard Martin. *The HeartMath Solution*. San Francisco: HarperSanFrancisco, 1999.

Fisichella, Anthony J. *Metaphysics: The Science of Life*. St. Paul, MN: Llewellyn Publications, 1988.

Hawkins, David R. *Power vs. Force: The Hidden Determinants of Human Behavior*. Carlsbad, CA: Hay House, 1995.

Institute of Noetic Sciences and Captured Light Industries, *What the Bleep Do We Know? Study Guide*. Published online 2005 at *www.noetic.org/*.

Jarow, Rick *Creating the Work You Love*. Rochester, VT: Destiny Books, 1995.

Jaworski, Joseph, *Synchronicity: The Inner Path of Leadership*. San Francisco: Berrett-Koehler Publishers, 1996.

Laszlo, Ervin. *Science and the Akashic Field*. Rochester, VT: Inner Traditions, 2004.

McTaggert, Lynne. *The Field: The Quest for the Secret Force of the Universe*. New York: Quill, 2003.

Ray, James A. *The Science of Success*. LaJolla, CA: SunArk Press, 1999.

Seale, Alan. *Soul Mission*Life Vision*. Boston: Red Wheel, 2003.

————. *Intuitive Living: A Sacred Path*. Boston: Weiser Books, 2001.

Senge, Peter, and C. Otto Scharmer, Joseph Jaworski, Betty Sue Flowers. *Presence: Human Purpose and the Field of the Future*. Cambridge, MA: The Society for Organizational Learning, 2004.

Three Initiates, *The Kybalion: A Study of the Hermetic Philosophy of Ancient Egypt and Greece*. Chicago: The Yogi Publication Society, 1912.

Wolf, Fred Alan. *Taking the Quantum Leap*. New York: Harper & Row, 1981.

Zukav, Gary. *The Dancing Wu Li Masters*. New York: Perennial Classics, 2001.

Alan Seale is a highly sought after leadership and transformation coach. He has led workshops and keynote presentations at the Kripalu Center in Lenox, MA; the International Coach Federation annual conference in St. Louis, MO; the South Bay Organizational Development Network in Silicon Valley, CA; and similar events nationally. He is the author of *Intuitive Living* and *Soul Vision*Life Mission*. He lives in Rochester, New York. Visit him online at *www.alanseale.com*.

Photo credit: Maureen Edwards

TO OUR READERS

Weiser Books, an imprint of Red Wheel/Weiser, publishes books across the entire spectrum of occult and esoteric subjects. Our mission is to publish quality books that will make a difference in people's lives without advocating any one particular path or field of study. We value the integrity, originality, and depth of knowledge of our authors.

Our readers are our most important resource, and we appreciate your input, suggestions, and ideas about what you would like to see published. Please feel free to contact us, to request our latest book catalog, or to be added to our mailing list.

Red Wheel/Weiser, LLC
665 Third Street, Suite 400
San Francisco, CA 94107
www.redwheelweiser.com